# Table of Contents (Server+ 2012 Edition)

## CONTENT UPDATES

ExamREVIEW is an independent content developer not associated/affiliated with CompTIA. The exam described is the trademark of CompTIA. We at ExamREVIEW develop study material entirely on our own. Our material is fully copyrighted. Braindump is strictly prohibited. We provide essential knowledge contents, NOT any generalized "study system" kind of "pick-the-right-answer-every time" techniques or "visit this link" referrals.

All orders come with LIFE TIME FREE UPDATES. When you find a newer version of the purchased product all you need to do is to email us and we will send you the updated version BY EMAIL free of charge.

Our email address: Michael@examreview.net

# About this book

The Server+ exam is computer based - no need for paper and pencil at all. It has multiple choice questions only. It aims to measure foundation level server skills and knowledge.

Topics that have to be dealt with in the exam include:

- System Hardware

- Software

- Storage

- IT Environment

- Disaster Recovery

- Troubleshooting

Although you don't have to be A+ certified in order to go for Server+, knowledge covered by the A+ certification is essential. After all, we are dealing with PC-like X86 based servers here.

We give you knowledge information relevant to the exam specification. To be able to succeed in the real exam, you'll need to apply your earned knowledge to the question scenarios. Many of the exam questions are written to be less straight forward. They tend to be framed within the context of short scenarios.

The exam is not too difficult. However, coverage is very comprehensive – a wide range of topics are presented in the official topic list. The exam does not ask you to answer hundreds of questions. In other words, only a small fraction of the official topics will be presented.

**To succeed in the exam, you need to read as many reference books as possible. There is no single book that can cover everything!**

**This ExamFOCUS book focuses on the more difficult topics that will likely make a difference in exam results. The book is NOT intended to guide you through every single official topic. You should therefore use this book together with other reference books for the best possible preparation outcome.**

# Server roles, capacity planning, tuning and maintenance

## Overview

A computer network is a system for communication between individual computers. These networks may be fixed via cabling or temporary via modems or other remote connection methods. A server is a computer on a network that manages network resources. A file server is a computer and storage device dedicated to storing files. A print server is a computer that manages one or more printers. A network server is a computer that manages network traffic. A database server is a computer system that processes database queries.

## Servers VS Desktops

**Servers are mostly dedicated, that they would perform no other tasks besides their assigned server tasks. You do not do your work on the server. You do your work on your own desktop PC, then save your works on the server.** The basic components of a server and a regular PC are the same. The two primarily differ in these aspects:

| | |
|---|---|
| ● Intended use | ● Number of processors |
| ● Workload | ● Amount of RAM |
| ● Physical storage | ● Specialized storage |
| | ● Maintenance |

**High-end servers perform very specific jobs, and that their designs always require fault-free operation - the server is not expected to crash at all.**

## Server roles

The minimum specification for a server hardware would depend largely on the role the server is going to play, the processes and services that will run on it, and the number of users it will have. Also note that a server can be configured to perform specific roles. The applications that the server runs determine the particular server's role. For a server to undertake a role, additional services and features will have to be installed. This is why the server's role is the single most important factor in determining the hardware that a server requires. Typical server roles include:

- Backup server

- Database server

- Domain controller

- File server

- Print server

- RAS server

- Web server

- Email server

Do note that in the world of Windows computing, a domain controller stores a copy of Active Directory and maintains the directory data store. Active Directory aims to provide a centralized repository of information for securely managing an organization's resources.

## Hardware capacity planning

Server load is almost always driven by peak users. Practically, server load is difficult to predict so live testing would be the best way to determine the hardware capacity required.

Generally, server hardware can almost always benefit from having more RAM. This is due to the fact that as soon as the operating system has to write data onto the drive the server will experience a performance drop. The choice of processor, on the other hand, is usually dependant on how intensively the server is used. The nature of workload has to be considered too. For example, a file server will not require anywhere near the same processor power as a database server since file access doesn't require much computation; it does require faster I/O.

## Storage

In terms of storage, SCSI disks are reliable, and that most of them have the ability to mark bad sectors as unreadable via the SCSI adaptors disk utilities.

HOWEVER, they are very expensive. SATA and PATA hard drives are cheaper but are less reliable when under high workload.

Talking about speed, traditional SCSI technology (all the way up to SCSI-3 standard) does not really keep up with the serial technologies being developed for PC. SAS Serial Attached SCSI is a newer SCSI standard with a much higher transfer speed (6Gb/sec or so).

The SATA cable is 7 pins wide. The IDE Ribbon Cable is 40 pins wide. IDE transfers data at speeds of 5MB/sec up to 133MB/Sec (ATA100/133). SATA's transfer speeds range from 150MB/sec to 300MB/sec (SATA II). SATA II supports NCQ as well. NCQ Native Command Queuing refers to the use of a special algorithm for determining the most efficient order in which to perform read and write operations.

## RAID

A RAID configuration can provide additional protection against data loss by mirroring the data on multiple hard disks, thus protecting yourself from disk failure. The more disks a server has the better the redundancy. Hardware RAID generally performs better than software RAID since hardware RAID has a dedicated chip for managing the RAID operation:

- RAID 0 has two disks. Data is distributed to two disks for taking advantage of higher disk read/write speeds. If one disk fails, there is no way you can recover the data.

- RAID 1 has two disks. Data is written to two disks so if one disk fails you still have an exact copy on the other.

- RAID 5 has three disks minimum. The disks keep both data and parity information. If any one disk fails, it can be replaced and the data can be recovered.

- RAID 6 has four disks minimum. Data and the parity information is distributed to all disks, with parity data distributed twice. If any two disks fail, the data can still be recovered.

Advanced servers always use ECC memory. ECC memory is error correcting code memory. This memory system will test and correct any errors in memory without involving the processor. The way it works is through a checksum - it generates a checksum when data is loaded in memory, and the checksum is recomputed when being unloaded. If an error is detected, it will be automatically corrected.

## Server performance monitoring and tuning

To troubleshoot performance problems you must monitor - that is, to track down the problem using the available monitoring resources. If you do not monitor, you will have no way solving the problem. To achieve the best possible performance, you need to identify the performance bottlenecks and minimize the time it takes for the server to process user requests. Generally, you need to:

- monitor memory and CPU usage

- resolve hardware or software issues that may be causing problems - sometimes it is a hardware problem. Sometimes it may be a software one...

- before you start monitoring, first establish baseline performance metrics for the server by measuring server performance at various times and under different load conditions so proper comparison can be made.

A comprehensive monitoring plan should cover these:

- what server resources should be monitored

- what filter to use for reducing the amount of information collected

- what performance counters to use for watching resource usage

- what data to log

Generally speaking, these are what you should watch for:

- Memory Usage - you want to know the amount of memory the services need relative to themselves and to the operating system memory. Both your operating system and your services should have sufficient memory to use.

- CPU usage - high CPU utilization rates means the processor is underpowered.

- Disk I/O performance - when there is too much I/O you may need to add more RAM and at the same time upgrade to a high performance disk system

- Blocking Locks - this happens when a process keeps another from accessing the resource. This is often a problem specific to the service in use.

If you are using Windows, these are the tools you can use to monitor:

- Performance Monitor

- Access logs

- Event logs

The Playback tool suite has two components which are useful for monitoring web site performance. They are PLAYBACK.EXE and RECORDER.DLL. RECORDER.DLL records ongoing activity while PLAYBACK.EXE plays back the recorded activity. Web Application Stress Tool can also be used to simulate Web activity for stress testing.

**Server maintenance schedule**

Periodic maintenance on server systems are preventive measures that are mandatory due to the possible needs for:

- Installation of patches

- Hardware upgrades

- Software patches and upgrades

- Software and component installations

- Re-configurations

- Server reboots

- Availability testing

These are the common server maintenance tasks:

- Check disk space usage

- Clean out temporary files

- Update Antivirus and Anti-Spyware software

- Check backup of system state

- Check all scheduled tasks

- Check local daily backup to external hard disk

- Check daily web based backup if any

- Check e-mail mailbox usage

- Check event logs

- Check surge protectors and UPS systems

- Check weekly drive imaging if any

## Server troubleshooting

The first step in server troubleshooting is to identify the environment in which the problem occurred. This may include both the hardware and software versions as well as any currently applied patches.

You should know the operating system version and most recently applied patches for each of the systems involved, as well as their security details. Additionally, you need to figure out the version and patch level of any additional software packages that are interacting with your server. In many cases, errors are the results of missing service pack or outdated operating system level.

With sufficient information on hand, you now have to clearly identify the actual problem. Your focuses should be on addressing these:

- What had happened

- Where…

- When…

- What effect it had on the server and the computing environment

Then you need to identify the full scope of the problem. To do so you need to detect a behavioral pattern for the problem. Ask yourself these questions:

- How many servers or components are experiencing the error?

- What is the impact of a single error?

- How many errors on each server or component?

- What is the total impact?

- Can the problem be reproduced in a test environment?

- Does the problem recur periodically?

- Has the problem spread to other components or servers?

After identifying the problem and scope, it is time to identify the potential cause(s). The key question to ask - what changes have been made to the server recently?

Once you have picked and applied a solution, make sure you verify that it is a viable solution and not just a temporary fix. You don't attack just the symptom. You need to attack the root cause of the problem. If you can confirm that you have identified the true cause, then you should identify steps to eliminate the potential for a repeat of that problem.

## Review Questions:

1, What determines a server's role?

2, Generally, server hardware can almost always benefit from having more RAM. Is it true?

3, Compare RAID 0 with RAID 1.

4, Compare SCSI disk with SATA disk.

5, Describe how ECC memory works.

6, RAID 6 requires how many disks at the least?

7, What is NCQ?

8, Compare SATA with EIDE.

## Answers:

*1, A server can be configured to perform specific roles. The applications that the server runs determine the particular server's role.*

*2, Generally, server hardware can almost always benefit from having more RAM. This is due to the fact that as soon as the operating system has to write data onto the drive the server will experience a performance drop.*

*3, RAID 0 has two disks. Data is distributed to two disks for taking advantage of higher disk read/write speeds. If one disk fails, there is no way you can recover the data. RAID 1* has two disks. Data is written to two disks so if one disk fails you still have an exact copy on the other.

4, SCSI disks are reliable, and that most of them have the ability to mark bad sectors as unreadable via the SCSI adaptors disk utilities. HOWEVER, they are very expensive. SATA and PATA hard drives are cheaper but are less reliable when under high workload.

5, ECC memory is error correcting code memory. This memory system will test and correct any errors in memory without involving the processor. The way it works is through a checksum - it generates a checksum when data is loaded in memory, and the checksum is recomputed when being unloaded.

6, RAID 6 has four disks minimum. Data and the parity information is distributed to all disks, with parity data distributed twice.

7, NCQ Native Command Queuing refers to the use of a special algorithm for determining the most efficient order in which to perform read and write operations.

8, The SATA cable is 7 pins wide. The IDE Ribbon Cable is 40 pins wide. IDE transfers data at speeds of 5MB/sec up to 133MB/Sec (ATA100/133). SATA's transfer speeds range from 150MB/sec to 300MB/sec (SATA II).

# Operating systems

An operating system is the most important program that runs on a computer. Every computer must have an operating system to run other programs. It performs all the basic tasks, such as recognizing input from the keyboard, sending output to the display screen, keeping track of files and directories on the disk, and controlling peripheral devices of all kinds. Windows, Linux and Mac OSX are all examples of operating system.

The most popular server operating systems in the market include:

- Windows Server

- Linux

- Unix (Solaris, SCO Unix...etc)

- Netware

**Server operating system differs from a desktop one in that it is often optimized for handling processes that run behind the scenes (the background processes). In the world of Unix, a daemon refers to a type of background process that runs continually in the background.**

A file system is a data structure that an operating system uses to keep track of files on a disk or partition; the way the files are organized on the disk. You can think of the file system as a hierarchical collection of files and directories that make up an organized, structured set of stored information you can retrieve if needed or wanted. You should create folders when you want to organize your data into groups and to store data hierarchically on the hard disk. For example, if you wanted to store photos, you may want to create a folder on your hard disk called MY BEAUTIFUL PHOTOS and store all of them in there. You may want to go further and create subdirectories to store groupings within this like one folder for LOVER and another for SCENES.

Windows Explorer is the Windows Shell interface to the desktop and filing system. It is split into two panes with a collapsible hierarchy showing the directory structure on the left side, and a sub window displaying the current folder's contents at the right. The Computer Manager, on the other hand, is where all your computer management tools reside within a convenient interface.

Partitioning refers to the process of creating virtual markers that separate drive letters in DOS and Windows. There are 3 types of partitions: primary, extended & logical. A partition table is the list of what partitions have been configured on a drive. The Disk Defragmenter can consolidate fragmented files and folders on your computer's hard disk, so that each occupies a single, contiguous space on the volume. As a result, your system can gain access to your files and folders and save new ones more efficiently. The backup and restore utility (and other disaster recovery utilities) can help you keep your data safe. If you have a disk failure, if you accidentally delete data, the backup and restore utility can help you to get back on track.

On the other hand, the Disk Cleanup Wizard can check a specified volume and estimates the amount of disk space it might be able to recover and let you use once completed. Attrib is a command line utility that can be used to view or alter file permissions, including A: Archive; R: Read Only; S: System; and H: Hidden.

## Review Questions:

1, What are the functions of an operating system?

2, What is partitioning for? What is a partition table?

3, What utility can you use to consolidate fragmented files?

4, What is a daemon?

## Answers:

*1, Every computer must have an operating system to run other programs. It performs all the basic tasks, such as recognizing input from the keyboard, sending output to the display screen, keeping track of files and directories on the disk, and controlling peripheral devices of all kinds.*

*2, Partitioning refers to the process of creating virtual markers that separate drive letters in DOS and Windows. There are 3 types of partitions: primary, extended & logical. A partition table is the list of what partitions have been configured on a drive.*

*3, The Disk Defragmenter can consolidate fragmented files and folders on your computer's hard disk, so that each occupies a single, contiguous space on the volume. As a result, your system can gain access to your files and folders and save new ones more efficiently.*

*4, In the world of Unix, a daemon refers to a type of background process that runs continually in the background.*

# Internet, virtual office and electronic business

### Internet

Internet is the global network that connects millions of computers around the globe. Each Internet connected computer, called a host, is an independent entity even though they are kind of being connected together via different kinds of connection methods.

### Web

The World Wide Web (WWW) is the system of interlinked, hypertext documents (web pages) that can be accessed via the Internet through the use of web browser software. Web pages are often created with HTML – the hypertext markup language.

### Intranet

Intranet is a special variation of the internet that is accessible only by the organization's members, employees, or others with authorization. An intranet's Web sites look and act just like those regular Web sites, but the firewall devices surrounding the intranet fend off all unauthorized access attempts.

To connect to the internet, your office may have a direct Internet connection, which is a connection hardwired to an Internet server. You can be connected over a network, but it still means there is a hardwired line somewhere in your office to an Internet server. On the other hand, in a virtual office setup you may have a remote or dial-in connection. This is the kind of connection that goes via the phone lines and modems to a commercial Internet Service Provider.

## Browsing

To read web pages, you need to use a web browser software. Browsers are basically software that allows you to search for and view various kinds of information on the Web. Netscape and Internet Explorer are famous examples of browser software.

Web pages are mostly written in HTML. HTML stands for Hyper Text Markup Language. It is the primary programming language used to write content on the Web. On the browser you type in a unique web site address (something like www.hello.com) and the browser will take you there.

## Languages

Modern web pages may be created via different languages. Extensible Markup Language (XML) is a general-purpose markup language which is "extensible" as it allows users to define their own tags. With XML different commercial systems may communicate so that the exchange of information can become much easier.

Java is a programming language. It is also a computing platform. It allows complex programs to run through the web. In fact it also runs on mobile and TV devices. Do note that Java is a technology of Sun Microsystems.

Active Server Pages ASP is a server side scripting engine that enables the creation of dynamic and interactive web pages. ASP.NET is a comprehensive web application framework. ASP is a technology of Microsoft.

Ajax represents a broad group of web technologies that may be used to implement a web application that communicates with a server in the background, without the need to interfere with the current state of the web page. Simply put, a AJax web application may request only the content that needs to be updated, thus capable of drastically reducing bandwidth usage and load time.

A URL (Uniform Resource Locator) is the unique address for a file that is accessible on the Internet. This is the most common way to get to a Web site. For example, www.hello.com/howareyou.htm is a URL.

**Portal**

Enterprise Information Portals are special web based infrastructure which allow enterprise employees, partners and customers to search and access corporate information. You may think of it as a gateway for users to log into and retrieve corporate information, company history and other informational resources. You may in fact develop different portals based on business structure and strategic focus, for example:

- business-to-employee electronic commerce (B2E)

- business-to-consumer (B2C)

- business-to-dealer/distributor (B2D)

- business-to-business (B2B)

- business-to-government (B2G)

## EDI

Short for Electronic Data Interchange, EDI refers to the transfer of data between different companies using computer networks. The EDI standards that are commonly in use nowadays are collectively known as the X12 standards. Note that EDI and Internet can be two totally different things - EDI may or may not run on the internet.

## E-business

Electronic Business ("e-Business") may be thought of as the business process that relies on an automated information system running over the web. Comprehensive E-business infrastructure often involves business processes spanning the entire value chain, including electronic purchasing and supply chain management, processing orders electronically, handling customer service, and cooperating with business partners.

## Virtual office

A virtual office describes shared office services, which would normally includes business address, mail & courier services, phone services, fax services, answering services, web-hosting services, and meeting & conference facilities. Simply put, if you work from your home utilizing a computer, modem, fax machine, email or other electronic means to perform your job and communicate with your place of employment instead of actually attending the office, you are working in a virtual office.

Modern virtual offices work extensively through the internet. Collaboration through the internet is possible with advanced internet software such as Netmeeting, chat rooms, discussion boards, video conferencing ...etc. Working online this way can eliminate distance and reduce the costs of information exchange substantially.

## VPN

Short for virtual private network, a VPN is a network that is constructed by using public wires to connect hosts in different geographic locations. VPN systems use encryption and other security mechanisms to ensure that only authorized users can access the network and that the data being transmitted cannot be intercepted.

## Email

There are several similarities between email and regular snail mail. Both need to have a unique address. And both need to be "sent" and "picked up". The difference is that with email everything takes place electronically. Email addresses are unique. The domain part of the addresses actually determines what post office the mail will be sent to for delivery. Email has a unique post office, which is the email server.

Each email server has a unique name. When you send your email the last part of the address after the @ is the server address. You do need several things to send and receive email. You need an Internet connection, an email account, and also an email software package. When using email for communication, you want to pay attention to the so called email etiquette ("netiquette").

Remember, the immediacy of email has made it a more informal form of communication. Therefore, senders often write on the fly with little thought of how the message might be interpreted. You want to make sure you know whom you are replying to. because written messages do not convey the differences between fact, opinion or emotion, it would be a good idea to label opinions, reactions, or emotions using emotocons (or "smileys" -> somethign like this: :-) traditional smile :-D Toothy grin ;-) winking ). Never type in all upper case as IT MEANS YOU ARE SHOUTING. And keep in mind, even though email messages are like conversation, they are in fact quite permanent. Also, your message can be forwarded to known or unknown third parties!

## Review Questions:

1, What is the use of an URL?

2, Describe XML.

3, Traditional web pages are mostly written in which language?

4, What is Ajax and what is so special about it?

## Answers:

1, A URL (Uniform Resource Locator) is the unique address for a file that is accessible on the Internet. This is the most common way to get to a Web site. For example, www.hello.com/howareyou.htm is a URL.

2, Extensible Markup Language (XML) is a general-purpose markup language which is "extensible" as it allows users to define their own tags. With XML different commercial systems may communicate so that the exchange of information can become much easier.

3, Web pages are mostly written in HTML. HTML stands for Hyper Text Markup Language. It is the primary programming language used to write content on the Web.

4, Ajax represents a broad group of web technologies that may be used to implement a web application that communicates with a server in the background, without the need to interfere with the current state of the web page. Simply put, a AJax web application may request only the content that needs to be updated, thus capable of drastically reducing bandwidth usage and load time.

# Hardware and devices

## Printers and scanners

You use a printer to produce hard copies out of your computer files. The major types of printers include laser printer, inkjet printer (including bubble jet printers), dot matrix printer and thermal printer. Dot Matrix printers are no longer popular. They work by firing pins at a ribbon. Thermal printers can produce hard copy through heating up the coated thermochromic paper. Inkjet printers use liquid ink-filled cartridges. The ink cartridge will allow for a force out and spray of electrostatic-charged droplets of ink onto a page. Laser printers, on the other hand, are toner based. They need time to 'warm up' if first turned on in order to get the fusing stage ready. Most laser printers support PostScript, which combines the best features of printers and plotters for producing high quality line art.

PostScript is a page description language in the electronic and desktop publishing areas. On the other hand, Dots per inch (DPI) is a measure of spatial printing / video dot density in the number of individual dots that can be placed within the span of a linear inch. The DPI value often indirectly correlates with image resolution. In any case, for any printer to work with your PC there must be a software that converts your application data to an acceptable format. This software effectively allows your applications to do printing without knowing the tech details of your physical printer. This is what a printer driver is all about.

A scanner is a computer device that can read printed text graphics and translate the information into a form the computer can read and store. It works by digitizing an image. The resulting matrix of bits (which is known as a bit map) can be stored in a file, displayed on a screen, or manipulated by software programs. Since scanners would not distinguish text from illustrations, you cannot directly edit text that has been scanned. To edit text scanned by the scanner, you need to use an optical character recognition (OCR) system to translate the image into text characters that can be read by your word processors. The scan resolution determines the file size and quality.

A flatbed scanner is composed of a glass pane, under which there is a bright light which illuminates the pane, and a moving optical array in scanning. A hand held document scanner is a manual device that is dragged across the surface of the image to be scanned. Scanning documents like this would require a steady hand. Scanner resolution is measured in pixels per inch (ppi), describe the resolution in the unit of pixels. To illustrate, a 100x100-pixel image that is printed on a 1-inch square is said to have 100 pixels per inch.

## Storages

A CD-ROM (compact disk read-only memory) is an optical read-only storage medium based on the original digital audio format first developed for audio CDs. Other formats such as CD-R, or CD recordable, and CD-RW, or CD rewritable, are basically the "writable" version of this form of storage medium. Note that CD based medium comes in a standard size of 700MB capacity. DVD (digital versatile disk), on the other hand, is a high capacity CD. Flash memory media (such as CF card and SD card) uses a special type of solid state memory chip that requires no power to maintain its contents. Flash memory can be easily moved from digital cameras to notebook or desktop computers and can even be connected directly to photo printers or self-contained display units. Flash memory card readers usually connect to the PC via USB.

A Write Once Read Many WORM drive is a special kind of data storage device where information, once saved, can never be modified. Reading is unlimited but writing is once only. They are pretty useful for archiving information when users need the security of knowing the information they look for has not been tampered with.

## System components

One most basic system components of a computer is the keyboard which is the primary input device. It is used for entering commands and data into the system. Mice come in many shapes and sizes from many manufacturers, and can usually connect to the computer through a serial interface, a PS2 mouse port, or a USB port. Many other types of input devices are available, such as joysticks, steering wheels, game pads, and pen tablets. These devices are usually connected to the PC via USB.

Universal Serial Bus (USB) is an expansion bus that allows up to 127 devices to be simultaneously connected to a single port. USB 2.0 offers a much higher data rate but is still compatible with USB 1.1. USB 3.0 can support a max transmission speed of up to 5 Gbit/s with the use of professional equipments. As specified in IEEE 1394 High Performance Serial Bus,

FireWire is similar to USB in use and it runs much faster than USB 1.0. In fact, FireWire can support up to 63 peripherals in a tree or daisy-chain topology and at the same time allow for peer-to-peer device communication.

There are many other devices that can be installed peripherally into a PC. Some of these include: bar code readers; multimedia devices; biometric devices; interactive devices and drawing tablets. Printers, scanners, copiers, faxes and external flash card readers are also examples of input devices that are of practical use. Sound cards provide audio output to the speaker or headphone devices and also accept input from microphones and external audio sources such as musical instruments and audio capturing devices.

## Laptops

Laptops are way smaller and since most devices are built-in to the main board they are much less upgradeable. This is especially true since manufacturers often prefer proprietary design rather than standard format. Still, they offer much better mobility than their desktop counterparts. Personal Computer Memory Card International Association (PCMCIA) is the standard for expansion cards on laptops. The corresponding expansion cards are often called PC Cards. **Laptops can never serve as servers. They can only serve as clients.**

## Display

Liquid crystal display (LCD) is a flat display panel commonly found on laptops. Older laptop screens deployed a passive matrix architecture - one that employs double-layer STN (DSTN) technology, which produce slow response time yet poor contrast in image display quality. Newer laptops use thin-film transistors (TFTs) as a form of Active-matrix display for much sharper and quicker image display.

Note that typical LCD displays offer a lower contrast ratio as well as slower response time. Some LCD display panels also had a very limited viewing angle. However, as the technology is getting mature, newer LCD displays can provide much better display quality. LED screens are LCDs that make use of a series of Light Emitting Diodes to backlight the LCD panel. LED backlighting is either direct or edge. Direct lighting can increase contrast levels, while edge lighting can make the screen very thin.

## Imaging Technologies and reprographic processes

An imaging system converts paper documents to electronic files. Item processing imaging systems (IPIS) are generally high speed systems (up to 1,850 documents per minute, or dpm) designed to capture checks and other items in the data processing environment. Document management imaging systems (DMIS) are generally low-speed systems (approximately 10–200 dpm) designed to capture a range of documents. Computer output to laser disk (COLD) is the computer process that outputs electronic records and printed reports to laser disk instead of a printer.

Digital imaging (aka digital image acquisition) is all about the creation of digital images from a physical object. The term often covers the processing, compression, storage, printing, and display of such images. On the other hand, Digital image processing is about the use of computer algorithms for performing image processing on digital images

Reprography refers to the reproduction of graphics through mechanical or electrical means (photography, xerography and the like). Reprography is popular for catalogs and archives, as well as in the architectural, engineering, and construction industries. Xerography is also known as electrophotography, which is a patented photocopying technique relying on the combination of electrostatic printing and photography. A photocopier is a device that can be used to make paper copies of documents and other visual images quickly and cheaply. Most modern photocopiers use xerography as the technology behind the scene.

Photocopying material that is subject to copyright is subject to restrictions in most countries. The principle of fair use typically allows this type of copying for education and research purposes.

## Review Questions:

1, How does thermal printers work?

2, What does DPI measure?

3, FireWire can support up to how many peripherals in a tree?

4, Which technology standard allows up to 127 devices to be simultaneously connected to a single port?

5, Describe LED screens.


## Answers:

*1, Thermal printers can produce hard copy through heating up the coated thermochromic paper.*

*2, Dots per inch (DPI) is a measure of spatial printing / video dot density in the number of individual dots that can be placed within the span of a linear inch. The DPI value often indirectly correlates with image resolution.*

*3, FireWire can support up to 63 peripherals in a tree or daisy-chain topology and at the same time allow for peer-to-peer device communication.*

*4, Universal Serial Bus (USB) is an expansion bus that allows up to 127 devices to be simultaneously connected to a single port. USB 2.0 offers a much higher data rate but is still compatible with USB 1.1.*

*5, LED screens are LCDs that make use of a series of Light Emitting Diodes to backlight the LCD panel. LED backlighting is either direct or edge. Direct lighting can increase contrast levels, while edge lighting can make the screen very thin.*

# Advanced server technologies

## CISC vs RISC

A complex instruction set computing (CISC) makes use of a microprocessor instruction set architecture in which each instruction can execute several low level operations within a single instruction. Reduced instruction set computing (RISC) represents a different CPU design strategy - it emphasizes the use of simplified instructions.

RISC is based on the philosophy that "do less" can actually perform better. Zero Instruction Set Computer (ZISC) represents the extreme - it refers to the kind of chip technology which based on pure pattern matching and the almost total absence of micro- instructions. It relies heavily on massively hardwired parallel processing to achieve the speed and reliability desired.

## SMP and multi-core processors

Symmetric multiprocessing (SMP) is the kind of multiprocessor computer architecture which allows for two or more identical processors connected to a single shared main memory (remember those boards that let you plug in more than one CPUs?). Most multiprocessor systems today use a SMP architecture. Because they share the same main memory, bottleneck can still occur in the coordination of resources.

In the case of multi-core processors\*, the SMP architecture works at the cores, effectively treating them as separate processors in the same die. This technology is particularly popular in the PC market where cost of manufacturing is a major concern. Alternative architectures include asymmetric multiprocessing in which separate specialized processors are put in place for specific tasks, and computer clustered multiprocessing in memory availability to processors are specifically assigned.

To enjoy the benefits offered by these processors your OS must be capable of doing so (for example, multithreading may have to be supported, which allows application processes to be run in parallel). For PC level computers and servers, you need Linux, Windows (2000, XP, 2003, Vista, 2008 …etc), Solaris and the like. For higher end computers you need AS/400, Unix, OpenVMS and the like.

*\* A multi-core CPU (sometimes known as a chip-level multiprocessor) is a relatively new kind of CPU technology which combines two or more independent processor cores into a single die. For the PC market there are dual core processors as well as quad core processors being offered at pretty affordable price levels.*

With a dual-core configuration, an integrated circuit has two complete computer processors included together. These identical processors are placd side by side on the same die, each with its own path heading towards the system front-side bus. Multi-core is simply an expansion to the dual-core concept.

Do realize that optimization for the dual-core processor architecture would require both the operating system and the software applications to support thread-level parallelism TLP. This technology allows things to be done simultaneously.

## Virtualization

With Virtualization technologies a single physical device can act like having multiple physical versions of itself for sharing across the network. This is usually done with the help of multiple processor cores in the same processor die. Platform virtualization is performed by the host software. As a control program, this host creates a simulated computer environment for formulating a virtual machine to serve the guest software. With full virtualization, the virtual machine will simulate sufficient hardware functionality to allow an unmodified OS to run in isolation. On the other hand, with paravirtualization the virtual machine will not simulate hardware but will simply offer a special API to serve those modified guest OS.

## Motherboard RAID and RAID card

Motherboard RAID means RAID support is built-in to the motherboard. Most low cost motherboard RAID configurations support only RAID 0 and RAID 1. Some costlier boards do offer native support for RAID 5.

Modern RAID cards are either SATA based or SCSI based. With these cards, array management can be handled using its native utility or browser-based management solution. Do note that a high-bandwidth PCI Express based card needs not be fast since it can be a software based controller. True hardware based controller card has a dedicated chip which is way more expensive.

## 64bit computing

Modern servers are almost all 64-bit based. A 64-bit architecture can in theory more than double the amount of data a CPU can process on a per clock cycle basis. A performance increase is usually visible since a 64-bit CPU can handle more memory and larger files. In fact, a 64-bit architecture can allow a server to address up to 1 terabyte of RAM. With 32 bit, 4GB is max.

Do remember, benefits of a 64-bit architecture can be realized only if you are running a 64-bit operating system and 64-bit software and drivers. 32-bit software running on a 64bit platform will not go any faster.

## X86-64, Xeon and Core i7 based processors, and Turbo Boost

These are all Intel based processors: Core i3 is for entry-level consumer, Core i5 is for mainstream consumer, and Core i7 is for the business and high-end consumer markets for both desktop and laptop computers. Xeon is primarily for server and workstation. In fact, the Xeon CPUs generally have way more cache than their desktop counterparts.

x86-64 is an extension of the original x86 instruction set. It can now support way larger virtual and physical address spaces, and provides 64-bit general purpose registers.

Turbo Boost is a technology implemented by Intel only. It can be found in certain versions of their Core i5 and Core i7 processors. The feature enables an Intel based processor to run above its base operating frequency through the dynamic control of the CPU clock rate. The performance states can be defined by the Advanced Configuration and Power Interface ACPI specification.

## MCH, IMCH and DMI

In the past there were two chips in the core logic chipset on a PC motherboard, which are the northbridge and the southbridge. The need to separate different functions into the CPU, northbridge, and southbridge chips was due to the difficulty of integrating all components into one. Nowadays these functions tend to be migrated to the processor chip itself. Still, if a separate northbridge is employed in an Intel system it is being referred to as a memory controller hub (MCH), or integrated memory controller hub (IMCH) with the existence of an integrated VGA.

The Direct Media Interface (DMI) is a link between the Intel northbridge and the Intel southbridge on a motherboard. Server chipset using similar interface is known as the Enterprise Southbridge Interface (ESI).

## FSB, HT and QPI

A front-side bus FSB is a computer communication interface that carries data between the processor and the memory controller hub / the northbridge. Some computers also have a back-side bus for connecting the processor to the cache. Do note that speed of the front side bus is often regarded as a critical measure of computer performance.

HyperTransport HT is also known as Lightning Data Transport LDT. It is a technology feature for interconnecting processors via a bidirectional high-bandwidth low-latency point-to-point link. AMD actually uses HT to replace the Front-Side Bus in some of their newer microprocessors. Intel QuickPath Interconnect QPI is a point-to-point processor interconnect for replacing the Front Side Bus certain newer desktop platforms. A major goal is to compete with HyperTransport.

## Rackmount and blade enclosures

19-inch rack is the standardized enclosure for mounting multiple server modules. Each server module has a front panel which is 19 inches wide, with ears protruded on each side so the module can be fastened to the rack frame easily.

A blade server is a stripped down server computer in a modular designed enclosure. Such design has many components removed for saving space and minimizing power consumption. A blade enclosure can hold multiple blade servers while providing the necessary services such as power, cooling, networking, various interconnects and management.

## NAS and SAN

A NAS (network-attached storage) is a server dedicated to file sharing and nothing else. A SAN (Storage Area Network), on the other hand, is a high-speed network of shared storage devices which is available to all servers on the network. FCIP (Fibre Channel over IP) is a new network storage technology that combines the features of Fibre Channel and IP for connecting distributed SANs over long distances. It is in fact a tunneling protocol capable of providing congestion control and management.

## Clustering and NOS

Clustering represents the configuration where multiple computers are connected together in such a way that they run like a single computer. This configuration is most often deployed for parallel processing, load balancing and fault tolerance.

A NOS (network operating system) refers to a software based operating system that includes special functions for connecting computers and devices in a LAN. Technically speaking, Novell Netware, Microsoft Windows 2000/2003 Server, Linux and Unix are all examples of NOS. SNMP (Simple Network Management Protocol) refers to the set of protocols for managing complex networks. It works by sending protocol data units to different parts of a network. There are SNMP-compliant agents that store data (such as the health status) about themselves in the Management Information Bases and return this data to the management console. Such mechanism enables the central administration of a large network.

## Load balancing

One way to achieve server scalability is to have more servers added to the configuration so to distribute the load among the group of servers (server cluster). The load distribution among these servers is what we call load balancing. When there are multiple servers in a server group, network traffic needs to be evenly distributed among the servers.

Round Robin Load Balancing is primarily for DNS service. There is a built-in round robin feature of the BIND DNS server. It works by cycling through the IP addresses corresponding to a server group. Hardware load balancers are dedicated for routing TCP/IP packets to various servers in a cluster. They are more efficient and way costlier. Software Load Balancers are usually options that come shipped with expensive server application packages. Software based solutions usually cost less but are often application specific.

## Review Questions:

1, Compare CISC with RISC.

2, What is SMP? What is the benefit of implementing SMP?

3, How does virtualization work?

4, Compare NAS with SAN.

5, Describe FCIP.

6, What is the function of a NOS?

7, How does SNMP work?

## Answers:

1, *A complex instruction set computing (CISC) makes use of a microprocessor instruction set architecture in which each instruction can execute several low level operations within a single instruction. Reduced instruction set computing (RISC) represents a different CPU design strategy - it emphasizes the use of simplified instructions.*

2, *Symmetric multiprocessing (SMP) is the kind of multiprocessor computer architecture which allows for two or more identical processors connected to a single shared main memory (remember those boards that let you plug in more than one CPUs?). It allows for parallel processing.*

3, *With Virtualization technologies a single physical device can act like having multiple physical versions of itself for sharing across the network. This is usually done with the help of multiple processor cores in the same processor die.*

4, *A NAS (network-attached storage) is a server dedicated to file sharing and nothing else. A SAN (Storage Area Network), on the other hand, is a high-speed network of shared storage devices which is available to all servers on the network.*

5, *FCIP (Fibre Channel over IP) is a new network storage technology that combines the features of Fibre Channel and IP for connecting distributed SANs over long distances.*

6, *A NOS (network operating system) refers to a software based operating system that includes special functions for connecting computers and devices in a LAN.*

7, *SNMP (Simple Network Management Protocol) refers to the set of protocols for managing complex networks. It works by sending protocol data units to different parts of a network.*

# Basic PC based Server Hardware Know-How

## BIOS

BIOS stands for Basic Input/Output System, which is stored in ROM. BIOS is the first group of instructions that are available when the computer is turned on. It is used in the course of startup routine with a view to check out the system and prepare to run the hardware.

### Booting with a Boot Disk

If a computer fails to boot due to the problems caused by the Windows installation, you may boot the computer by using a bootable disk. The procedures are as follows:

- Create a boot disk in Windows.

- Turn off the computer.

- Insert the boot disk into the floppy drive.

- Start the computer.

If the system still fails to boot, it might be the problem that the BIOS is set to boot with the hard drive first rather than with the floppy.

A typical floppy drive internally consists of read/write heads, the head actuator, the spindle motor, circuit boards, and a disk controller.

## Changing BIOS Boot Sequence

In order to boot from disk instead of hard drive, you should:

- Turn off the computer.

- Remove the book disk from the floppy drive.

- Turn on the computer.

- Press the Delete key during the startup period.

- Change the boot priority of floppy drive to be of a higher value than that of the hard drive.

- Save & exit BIOS settings.

- Insert the boot disk into the floppy drive again.

- Reboot the computer.

## CMOS

CMOS (Complementary etal-oxide semiconductor) is a type of read-only memory chip. CMOS is used to store data that is read by the BIOS so as to obtain information on hardware configuration.

## Configuration Mismatch

CMOS is the first thing to check when a computer has errors. If a computer suddenly fails to run and generates an error message of "CMOS configuration mismatch", you should:

- Turn off the computer.

- Ensure the power-supply is disabled.

- Open the computer case.

- Carefully remove the CMOS battery.

- Use a multimeter to check the voltage of the CMOS battery.

## Battery

CMOS battery prevents information about the settings of the computer from getting lost when the power is off. It also maintains the external clock time. If a computer's CMOS information is erased, or the CMOS battery is broken, you should immediately replace the CMOS Battery with the procedures listed below:

Replacing the CMOS Battery can be done following these steps

- Turn off the computer.

- Open the computer case.

- Carefully remove the CMOS battery.

- Install the new CMOS battery.

- Set and save the date and time again.

- Turn on the computer and test it.

## Hardware Settings

Modifying hard drive settings in the CMOS is dangerous. You're only able to modify the LBA, CHS and ECHS (Extended CHS) settings in the CMOS. The sizing information of the hard drive (namely head, cylinders, and sectors configuration.) is retained by CMOS. (In fact, the values of the COM ports are retained by the CMOS as well).

## CMOS Errors

If you incorrectly modified the hard drive configuration, you may receive a CMOS checksum error in the course of boot up. You should therefore enter the CMOS setting screen and fix the wrong hard drive configuration.

If you lose the CMOS password, temporarily remove the CMOS battery and erase the CMOS information by shortening the corresponding jumper.

If you're unable to enter the CMOS setup screen even with the correct password, or that the computer freezes during memory count, you should immediately check the CPU and see if it is defective.

## CMOS Upgrade

Under the following circumstances, you may consider replacing the CMOS chip:

- The CPU is upgraded.

- The BIOS is upgraded.

- Failed motherboard battery.

- The CMOS chip is being affected by viruses.

Not all motherboards allow CMOS chip replacement. Some CMOS chips can be updated via software flash utilities.

## Processor

The CPU (central processing unit) is the heart of a computer in which arithmetic and logical operations are performed and instructions are decoded and executed. It controls and manages the entire operation of the computer.

The speed of a processor is a fairly simple concept. Speed is counted in megahertz (MHz) and gigahertz (GHz). Generally speaking, processor speed = core clock multiplier x bus speed. The most common CPU brands available are Intel and AMD.

## Processor Peripherals

A CPU fan is for cooling down the CPU. If the CPU fan is stopped, the following problems might occur:

- Physical CPU damage

- System lockup

- System automatic reboot

- OS restart failure

- POST failure

## BUS

A bus is a group of electrical conductors that are running parallel to each other. In general, they are found in multiples of eight (8, 16, 32, etc). The purpose of the bus is to provide a path to transmit data in the form of codes to every single part of the computer.

ISA is an outdated technology given today standard. It stands for Industry Standard Architecture. It is one of the most common expansion slot and card designs:

- The speed of a 8 bit ISA slot is 4.77 MHz.

- The speed of a 16 bit ISA slot is 8.33MHz.

PCI allows developers to develop expansion cards that would fully function in any PCI compatible system. It thus overcomes the limitations of ISA, EISA, MCA, etc, and it offers fast speed and good performance which satisfy today's needs. PCI-E is the latest generation of this technology. It is primarily for interfacing with high speed display card.

AGP (Accelerated Graphics Port) is designed by Intel. It is an expansion slot found on Intel Pentium II and later computers. AGP allows a separate data channel for video cards. A normal AGP bus has 32 bits.

## Memory

In the past, RAM (Random Access Memory) can be categorized into two types according to the access technology: Static Random Access Memory (SRAM) and Dynamic Random Access Memory (DRAM). Nowadays we mostly ignore SRAM and focus our attention on the various DRAM implementations. The most popular divisions of DRAM are: Synchronous DRAM (SDRAM), Rambus DRAM (RDRAM), Double Data Rate DRAM

(DDR DRAM) and DDR2 DRAM. The most popular types nowadays are DDR3 (DDR3 is required for the latest PC platforms).

## Video Adapter, DVI and HDMI

Video adapter cards provide video signal to the display device (the monitor). They often feature their own specialized Video CPU and Video RAM to speed up graphic rendering.

Modern display adaptors often come with support for DVI and even HDMI.

DVI shorts for Digital Visual Interface. It is a special video connector designed by the Digital Display Working Group for maximizing picture quality of digital projectors and LCD screens. Each DVI link has 4 twisted pair of wires for transmitting 24 bits per pixel. You do want to know that DVI uses both digital and analog transmission options via the same connector.

HDMI shorts for High-Definition Multimedia Interface. It is a digital interface that can be used with a HDTV to produce the best uncompressed digital picture possible. It sends audio and video signal in one cable, and is much faster than DVI.

## Video Card Memory

In the world of video display, VRAM, WRAM, and SGRAM are all known as "Video RAM":

- WRAM (Window Random Access Memory) is a high speed RAM that is cheaper than other video ram, yet it is slightly faster.

- VRAM can read/write to the I/O ports at the mean time. It is fast and expensive. VRAM is used you very high-quality video cards.

- SGRAM (Synchronous Graphics RAM) is mainly used in the mid-range of the video rams market. It is slower than both WRAM and VRAM.

VRAM and WRAM are the standard memory types for today's video cards, although SGRAM is seen as an increasingly popular alternative due to its high performance. If the video chip is built-in, there will be no separate video memory since the system memory will be shared with the video function.

**Refresh Rate**

The time it takes for a monitor's electron beam to draw the screen from top to bottom depends on how high the refresh rate is. It usually ranges from 60 to 80 Mhz.

Horizontal Refresh Rate (HRR) is the speed that the electron beam in a CRT completes a single horizontal trace. The higher the refresh rate, the more comfortable for your eyes. However, never set the refresh rate to a very high level, as it might cause the monitor to go blank when you try to change the resolution.

## Display Resolutions

Resolution is the method of measurement for the detail level of images produced by a monitor (or a printer). It is measured by a horizontal and vertical number of pixels for monitors. For a printer, resolution is mesured in dpi (dots per inch).

Any video resolution higher than 640 x 480 is considered as in the SVGA display mode. SVGA is the minimum standard nowadays. In order to run the display at a resolution of 1024 x 768 in 24 bit color (which is what most people prefer), the video adapter requires at least 4MB of memory. More memory is required if higher resolution and color depth are expected.

## Energy Star

An "Energy Star Compliant Monitor" is able to switch to lower power states when the signal of display does not change.

## Changing Resolutions

In order to change the display resolution, you need to:

- Ensure the latest video card driver is installed.

- Ensure the video card has the memory necessary to change to the resolution you desire.

- Ensure the video card is functioning properly.

Changing video resolution may lead to display failure. If this happens, you should press ALT + F4 + ENTER during system startup in order to boot Windows directly to safe mode and change the video resolution again.

**Sound Card Settings**

When installing a sound card, you should have set the IRQ, DMA, and I/O addresses by using the software provided by the manufacturer.

The following settings are used for common sound cards:

- IRQ - 5

- I/O Address - 220

- DMA - 1

- MIDI Address - 330

Built-in sound chip is become very popular these days – sound function is fully integrated into the motherboard so configuration is way less complicated.

MIDI stands for Musical Instrument Digital Interface. It permits a computer to communicate with musical devices. Speakers regenerate sound. Without a pair of speakers, there will be no sound available.

**Troubleshooting sound card via Device Manager**

A system will not be able to play sound:

- As the consequence of hardware conflict.

- When you are running Windows in Safe Mode.

You can find out if your sound card is working via the Device Manager.

To reach the **Device Manager** tab, click **Start – Settings – Control Panel – Systems – Device Manager**.

**Black Exclamation Point** - If there is a black exclamation point on a yellow field next to a sound card in the **Device Manager** tab, the sound card is not functioning properly. To fix such malfunctioning sound card, launch the

**Hardware Conflict Troubleshooter** from **Windows Help,** click the **Properties** section of the sound card and analyze the **Resources Panel** for conflicting resources settings.

A lot of the time the sound problems come from mis-configuraton by the user. Examples:

- You plug the left-speaker to the right jack and the right-speaker to the left jack

- You use an incorrect CD audio cable.

- You haven't turn on the speakers.

- You mute the sound.

In some rare cases, the user might accidentally mutes the system sound. To fix this problem, you should check the Volume Control Applet. If the sound device is somehow muted, simply clear the mute check box.

## I/O Addresses and DMA

I/O addresses are codes of 1s and 0s transmitted across the address bus by the CPU. The CPU identifies the device before any data is placed on the bus. DMA (Direct memory access) allows a peripheral device to access the memory directly. DMA speeds up the data transmission speed.

## PCMCIA

PCMCIA stands for Personal Computer Memory Card Interface Association. They are also known as PC Cards. PC Cards can be installed in Laptops or Notebook Computers.

There are three types of PC Cards, namely, Type 1, Type 2, Type 3. All PC Cards will be detected by Windows every time the system starts.

| Type | Features |
| --- | --- |
| Type 1 | Work only with memory expansion cards. They are 3.3 mm thick. |
| Type 2 | Support most types of expansion cards. They are 5 mm thick. |
| Type 3 | Support removable hard drives. They are 10.5 mm thick. (Introduced in 1992.) |

## USB

USB (Universal Serial Bus) is a new standard for external expansion bus that is popular for use with low-speed mass storage devices such as Zip drives, or external devices such as modems, printers, scanners and digital cameras. Note that

- It is the newest type of serial bus architecture.

- USB is slower than IEEE1394.

- All USB devices are Plug & Play. They can be connected as needed.

- All USB devices will only use ONE IRQ irrespective of how many USB devices are currently installed.

- All USB ports are able to provide power to the potential USB devices.

Installing a USB device generally involves these steps:

- Turn off the computer.

- Plug in the device.

- Turn on the computer.

- Run the Add/Remove Hardware wizard.

- Choose the "Have Disk" option.

- Choose the appropriate driver for the newly installed USB device.

- Reboot the computer.

If the operation system fails to recognize an USB device, the possible causes are:

- The cable is disconnected.

- The USB port is dirty or broken.

- The software driver is corrupted.

## Hard Drive

The basic physical construction of a hard disk drive consists of spinning disks with read/write heads that move over the disk surfaces to store and read data. Hard drives typically have 2 connectors, one for interfacing to the computer, and one for receiving power. There are two primary types of hard drives, which are EIDE (enhanced IDE) and SCSI. In the past, SCSI was the only choice for high performance systems. However, with the introduction of new IDE technologies like SATA, IDE based platforms are gaining popularity due to improved performance and lower cost.

## IDE, SATA and PATA

Most PCs use IDE or SATA hard drives. Most older servers use SCSI drives. The good thing about SATA is that it uses very thin cables. It also has an IDE emulation mode so its interface can operate as IDE for backward compatibility purpose.

**The problem with thick cables is that they fill up the chassis and block air flow.**

The Parallel ATA PATA standard predates the SATA by a decade. Normally, parallel devices should transfer data faster than series devices. In the case of PATA and SATA, SATA is actually way faster. Also, PATA uses wide cables and is bound to take a lot of space.

## Power Supply

The basic function of a power supply is to convert the type of electrical power available at the wall socket to the type that computer circuitry can use. The power supply in a conventional desktop system is designed to convert either 115 volt or 230 volt AC power into 12 volt DC power.

Server power supplies are rated based on their maximum output power. Power requirements for a desktop may range from 300 watts to 400+ watts. For servers you will need way more since a lot of devices may have to be supported.

Some servers have hot swappable power supplies (PSU) so you can pull it out while the server is still running. No downtime at all! If the server power supply has a redundant configuration, then it will simply pick up when the primary one fails, again without any downtime to the server.

**The benefits of a hot swappable power supply are redundancy and ease of replacement. The drawback is cost.**

## Compatibility problems

These are the more common compatibility issues:

- Not all processors are compatible with all motherboards.

- Motherboards tend to be quite selective on the speed and type of RAM module needed.

- Newer motherboards feature PCI-Express slots only while older motherboards offer a combination of ISA/AGP slots and regular PCI slots. Know the type of slots available before buying any add-on components.

Components may conflict for different technical reasons. If you boot into a blue screen or that the computer freezes, try to press F8 as you boot your system, then load Windows in Safe Mode, which will sidestep drivers and devices that are unnecessary for basic Windows operation. You may then isolate problems easily. You may also find a hardware compatibility list (HCL) very useful. It is a list of computer hardware proven to be compatible with a particular operating system. Each operating system has its own official HCL on its website.

## Review Questions:

1, What is the function of DVI?

2, HRR is a feature of which type of display monitor?

3, Why is it important to maintain the CMOS battery?

4, What are the valid types of PC Card?

5, What technology permits a computer to communicate with musical devices?

6, What are the pros of a hot swappable power supply?


## Answers:

*1, DVI shorts for Digital Visual Interface. It is a special video connector designed by the Digital Display Working Group for maximizing picture quality of digital projectors and LCD screens.*

*2, Horizontal Refresh Rate (HRR) is the speed that the electron beam in a CRT completes a single horizontal trace. The higher the refresh rate, the more comfortable for your eyes.*

*3, CMOS battery prevents information about the settings of the computer from getting lost when the power is off. It also maintains the external clock time.*

*4, There are three types of PC Cards, namely, Type 1, Type 2, Type 3. All PC Cards will be detected by Windows every time the system starts.*

*5, MIDI stands for Musical Instrument Digital Interface. It permits a computer to communicate with musical devices.*

*6, The benefits of a hot swappable power supply are redundancy and ease of replacement. The drawback is cost.*

# Software Licensing and Green Computing

## Freeware VS Shareware VS Opensource

Freeware refers to software which can be downloaded, used, and copied without restrictions. You may not have access to the source code though. Shareware allows you to download and try the software for free, but if you decide to keep using it then you are supposed to pay for it. Open source means that the source code is available to you and you are free to use, change, and re-distribute the source code.

## Licensing

To ensure you have licenses for all the software installed on the computer, these are the guidelines you should follow:

- Establish and maintain accurate software logs and inventories.

- Establish a baseline inventory of software currently in place, and conduct inventory reviews regularly.

- Only purchase software from a source authorized by the software publisher.

Software may be delivered in different ways. Some software products are available to download, while can be picked up at a store or delivered via courier. Different delivery modes may have different licensing requirements. In any case, when maintaining software inventory these should be tracked:

- product name, version number, and serial number

- date and source of software acquisition

- location of installation and the installation media

These are the guidelines to follow to avoid violating the license requirement:

- do not use one licensed copy to perform installation on multiple computers

- do not copy disks for distribution

- do not swap disks at wish

- do not use software after the expiration of the license

## DRM

DRM is not the same as software licensing. As an acronym for Digital Rights Management, it describes a number of techniques for restricting the free use and transfer of digital contents (mostly video and music files). In fact, many creators of eBooks are using DRM technologies to limit how many computers an ebook file can be viewed on.

## Green Computing

Green IT is also known as green computing. It describes the initiatives to use information technology in a more environmentally friendly manner. When buying new computer equipment, you should look for an EnergyStar rating. ENERGY STAR is a government-backed symbol for energy efficiency. For computer in particular, a full set of specification can be viewed via this URL:

http://www.energystar.gov/ia/partners/prod_development/revisions/downloads/computer/Version5.0_Computer_Spec.pdf

A computer can be in different operating modes. Off Mode refers to the power consumption level in the lowest power mode which cannot be switched off by the user when the computer is connected to the main electricity supply. Sleep Mode is a low power state that the computer is capable of entering automatically after a period of inactivity. Idle State describes a state in which the operating system activity is limited and no user activities are performed. Active State has active processing undergoing.

Typical Energy Consumption (TEC) is the method for testing and comparing the energy performance of computers. It uses a key criterion which is a value for typical annual electricity use measured in kilowatt-hours (kWh). For determining TEC levels, desktops and integrated desktops may qualify under Categories A, B, C, or D. For notebook computer there is no category D.

## Cloud Computing

Cloud computing is all about distributed computing. An application is built using resources from multiple services from the same or different locations. By knowing the endpoint to access the services, the user can use software as a service, much like utility computing. Behind the scene there are grids of computers and the user does not need to know the details of the background stuff.

Grid computing describes the act of sharing tasks over multiple computers. A computational grid works by applying the resources of multiple computers together to resolving a single problem. A private cloud is a cloud computing infrastructure operated solely for a single organization. **In any case, cloud computing is energy friendly because people are effectively sharing computing resources.**

## Green buildings

The US Department of Energy's Building Energy Codes Program (BECP) is in place to support increased energy efficiency in residential and commercial buildings, by helping to advance building energy codes. BECP works by coordinating with other government agencies, state and local jurisdictions, national code organizations, and industry to promote stronger building energy codes. It also helps states in adopting, implementing, and enforcing those codes. The Energy Conservation and Production Act (ECPA) requires that each US state certify that it has a commercial building code in place to meet or exceed ANSI/ASHRAE/IESNA Standard 90.1-1999.

ASHRAE 90.1 is believed to be the most commonly used energy code for commercial and other non-residential buildings in the US. The Model Energy Code (MEC, aka the International Energy Conservation Code IECC) is the most commonly used residential energy code by states, although the International Residential Code (IRC) is also used by some US states. The NFPA also has commercial and residential energy codes. These codes, however, are based on the ASHRAE Standards 90.1 and 90.2.

LEED shorts for Leadership in Energy and Environmental Design. It is an internationally-recognized green building certification system developed by the US Green Building Council (USGBC) in 2000 for providing building owners and operators with a framework to identify and implement practical and measurable green building design, construction, operations and maintenance solutions.

## ACPI

Advanced Configuration Power Interface ACPI is a specification which allows an operating system to control the power distribution to the various computer peripherals. It works by communicating with the BIOS and instruct the BIOS to power down certain peripherals if necessary. It has replaced an older standard known as APM (Advanced Power Management) on Windows.

## Computer disposal

When you need to dispose of a computer, ALWAYS remove all the data that is on it first. Merely calling the "delete" command or dragging files to the trash can would not really remove the data from the disk. Even a plain "format" command would not be sufficient. The most secure way to remove your data is to use a specialized disk wiping utility. You may also want to evaluate the relevant software license agreements to determine if they allow the transfer of software along with the computer.

Most environmental concerns with computers lie with the traditional kind of CRT monitor. In fact, the Resource Conservation and Recovery Act (RCRA) has included guidelines regarding the disposal of computer monitors. From an environmental perspective, it is always more preferable to delay disposal so to reduce the environmental impacts associated with PC manufacture.

You should consider whether disposal is really necessary and whether it is possible to extend the life of the computer. And there are some options you can use when disposal is not a good idea. They are reuse, recycle, and trade-in. It is believed that recycling is the best option for computers that are seriously aged or broken.

## RoHS

RoHS (Restriction of Hazardous Substances) Compliance refers to the EU directive 2002/95/EC on the restriction of the use of some hazardous substances in electronic equipments. It aims at reducing the amount of hazardous materials that enter the life cycle of an electronic product. 6 materials are listed as being restricted, although certain exemptions are available.

RoHS regulations went into effect back in 2006. From a manufacturer perspective, careful testing and documentation are required in accordance with RoHS Directive regulations. Waste electrical and electronic equipment (WEEE) is different - it aims to reduce the amount of electronics entering the landfills.

## Review Questions:

1, Describe sleep mode.

2, What is the key criterion of TEC?

3, What is the first thing that you should do when there is a need to dispose of a computer?

4, How does cloud computing support "software as a service"?

5, What is the primary purpose of RoHS?

6, What is the key difference between freeware and open source?

7, What is special about the shareware usage model?

8, DRM is commonly deployed for protecting:

## Answers:

*1, Sleep Mode is a low power state that the computer is capable of entering automatically after a period of inactivity.*

*2, Typical Energy Consumption (TEC) is the method for testing and comparing the energy performance of computers. It uses a key criterion which is a value for typical annual electricity use measured in kilowatt-hours (kWh).*

*3, When you need to dispose of a computer, ALWAYS remove all the data that is on it first. Merely calling the "delete" command or dragging files to the trash can would not really remove the data from the disk.*

*4, Cloud computing is all about distributed computing. An application is built using resources from multiple services from the same or different locations. By knowing the endpoint to access the services, the user can use software as a service, much like utility computing.*

*5, RoHS (Restriction of Hazardous Substances) aims at reducing the amount of hazardous materials that enter the life cycle of an electronic product.*

*6, Freeware refers to software which can be downloaded, used, and copied without restrictions. You may not have access to the source code though. Open source means that the source code is available to you and you are free to use, change, and re-distribute the source code.*

*7, Try before you buy. Shareware allows you to download and try the software for free, but if you decide to keep using it then you are supposed to pay for it.*

*8, As an acronym for Digital Rights Management, it describes a number of techniques for restricting the free use and transfer of digital contents (mostly video and music files). In fact, many creators of eBooks are using DRM technologies to limit how many computers an ebook file can be viewed on.*

# Network Infrastructure

A typical top down approach to network infrastructure design requires that you understand the constraints and objectives of network use as well as the applications and data on which your business relies upon on, before considering the viable tech options. It is therefore advisable that you start with the business objectives because your network has the most important mission of helping end users in achieving their business objectives.

Some vendors suggest a layered approach to infrastructure implementation. For example, Cisco recommends the use of modules for offering high availability and scalability as well as flexibility. According to the Cisco model, with a well formed hierarchical network there should 3 layers, which are the access, distribution, and core layers. They provide different functions, but they do not exist in clear and distinct physical entities. Other vendors provide similar references that are made under different names.

Regardless of the layers and hierarchies that are proposed, from a technical standpoint they all rely on the same underlying technologies. The major items you should are being introduced as follow.

## Open System Interconnect

It offers a 7 layer model which can be used as a guideline for systematic network design, management and troubleshooting.

- The Application Layer is responsible for identifying and establishing the availability of desired communication partner and verifying sufficient resources exist for communication.

- The Presentation Layer is responsible for presenting the data in standard formats and provides services such as data compression, decompression, encryption, and decryption.

- The Session Layer is responsible for coordinating communication between network nodes.

- The Transport Layer is responsible for flow control, with the primary aim of maintaining data integrity. Simply put, it works to ensure complete data transfer.

- The Network Layer has the primary responsibility of sending data packets from the source network to the destination network using a pre-specified routing method.

- The Data Link Layer is divided into the sub-layers of Logical Link Control (LLC) and Media Access Control (MAC). The LLC sub-layer handles tasks such as error control, flow control and framing, while the MAC sub-layer handles access to shared media.

- The Physical Layer allows the actual flow of signals.

- Routing takes place at layer 3. On the other hand, switching takes place at layer 2. Routing requires more complicated configuration (usually).

## LAN Networking

The characteristics that differentiate one LAN from another include topology, protocols and cable media. Major concerns for selecting a network topology include performance, security and scalability.

- The STAR topology is the most common for LAN. It has a central point (hub or switch) that connects all workstations on the LAN. If there is a break in a cable, only the computer on the involved segment is affected.

- The bus topology has a single cable that connects all workstations on the LAN. If one computer goes down, the entire network goes down too.

- In a token ring network, an electronic token is passed around the network for transmitting data. There is no contention for the network, but performance is poor.

- A mesh network has multiple paths to the same destination. It is very costly to build and maintain and is more common for large scale WAN implementations.

Ethernet describes LAN products that are covered by the IEEE 802.3 standard. Available data rates include 10 Mbps—10Base-T Ethernet, 100 Mbps—Fast Ethernet 1000 Mbps and 10,000Mbps—Gigabit Ethernet.

In a modern LAN you will find Unshielded Twisted Pair (UTP) cable everywhere. It has four pairs of wires twisted inside it for eliminating electrical interference. It usually works with RJ-45 connectors which have eight connector pins. You use a straight-through cable to connect the source and destination computers through a hub or a switch (a switch runs more efficiently than a hub). Shielded Twisted Pair cables are more expensive, so they are less popular. Transmission through fiber optics does not necessarily go faster, but there is less interference, and signals can go farther away without much losses (in theory there is no loss, in practice it is hard to say 100% no losses…).

A crossover cable has the standard RJ-45 cable between source and destination cross-connected so you may connect computer to computer directly without going through a hub or a switch.

Collision is used by Ethernet to control access and allocate shared bandwidth among stations that try to transmit at the same time on the same shared medium. Ethernet uses Carrier Sense Multiple Access/Collision Detect (CSMA/CD) as its collision detection method. On the other hand, wireless network uses Carrier Sense Multiple Access/Collision Detect (CSMA/CA) – CA means collision avoidance.

You may use volt-ohm meters and digital multimeters to measure physical layer cabling characteristics, which may include and may not limit to AC and DC voltage, current, resistance, capacitance, and cable continuity. You may also use cable testers, which can test and report on cable conditions such as near-end crosstalk, attenuation, and noise.

# Routing and switching

TCP/IP is the communication language of internet networking devices. It requires routing in order to reach the outside networks. In other words, you need to use router to connect different networks together. Routing table is the major element required for making routing decision by the routers. Main considerations while building this routing table may include Administrative distance and Metrics amidst others.

In a typical enterprise network, different roles require different types of routers and switches. One thing for sure - at the network edge (where your LAN meets the outside world) you will need to implement security features (such as packet filtering as a minimum).

A LAN switch typically provides many ports that connect different LAN segments, and a high-speed port that connects the LAN switch to other devices in the network. It offers dedicated bandwidth per port, and that each port may be configured to represent a different segment. Practically speaking, in a LAN you may have more concerns on switching than on routing as switching is often more efficient than routing for handling traffic use within a LAN environment.

Routing protocols are for routers to communicate with each others. RIP for dynamic routing configuration is easy to setup but offers poor scalability as it's mechanism is limited by hop counts (the route with the fewest number of hops is always the best route), thus is mostly for LAN use. OSPF is better for large network due to a more sophisticated mechanism (it determines the best route by taking into account bandwidth as well as other factors) but is more complicated to set up. BGP is strictly a routing protocol for WAN.

A VLAN refers to a group of computers on multiple LANs that are configured to communicate as if they were attached to the same wire, when in fact they are located on different LANs. VLAN capable switches or routers are needed to allow for this kind of logical connection. Since VLANs are based on logical connections, they are extremely flexible in terms of configuration and application.

**IP Addressing**

To build and run a large network, you will have to take care of IP addresses subnet configuration and possibly routing table configuration. You may as well want to deploy routing protocols. This holds true for both LAN and WAN.

An IP address is the unique number ID assigned to one network interface. It is 32 bit based (as per IPv4).A subnet is a portion of a network sharing a particular subnet address. The gateway address is the router's address.

In a Class A address, the first octet is the network portion. In a Class B address, the first two octets are the network portion. In a Class C address, the first three octets are the network portion. Multicast IP addresses are Class D IP addresses ranging from 224.0.0.0 to 239.255.255.255.

Classless Interdomain Routing improves both address space utilization and routing scalability by having an IP network represented by a prefix. It is not yet the mainstream in most small to mid size environments though. On the other hand, Variable Length Subnet Masks (VLSM) allows the use of a long mask on networks with few hosts and a short mask on subnets with relatively more hosts.

The IPv6 address space has 128 bits, which is broken down into eight groups of 16 bits. There are two major 64-bit parts, which are the network prefix (contains the registry, provider, subscriber ID, and subnet) that occupies the higher order groups of bits and the interface ID that occupies the lower bits.

DNS (Domain Name System) is for name resolution. DHCP (Dynamic Host Configuration Protocol) is for dynamic IP address configuration. In a modern network you will need them both for ease of administration and scalability. Do note that dynamic addresses allocation is best for frequently changing network topology with a large amount of clients. If you have very few clients, static naming may be acceptable.

DNS performs name-to-IP mapping per the request of the client devices. The DNS namespace must be planned. A common practice is to have one namespace for the internal network and another for external contact.

LDAP are the set of protocols for accessing information directories. It is based on the standards contained within the X.500 standard but is deliberately made simpler, so that's why it is sometimes called X.500-lite.

It is an open protocol, meaning applications have no need to worry about the type of server hosting the directory.

## Wireless Based Local Area Networking

Wireless network relies on RF (Radio Frequency) to function. RF represents any frequency within the electromagnetic spectrum that is associated with radio wave propagation. Most wireless technologies for LAN use are based on RF field propagation. Potential sources of RF interference are microwave ovens, wireless phones, Bluetooth enabled devices and other wireless LANs.

A RF setup involves two parts, which are the transmitter and the receiver. The transmitter takes and encodes the message onto a sine wave for transmission. The receiver receives the radio waves and decodes accordingly. Do remember, Radio transmission ALWAYS requires a clear path between antennas (line of sight LOS).

IEEE 802.11 defines protocol for Ad-hoc and client/server networks. In particular it defines specifications for the physical layer and the Media Access Control layer.

A client/server based wireless network uses an access point to control the allocation of transmit time for all wireless stations. The access point is often the target of attackers.

Wired Equivalent Privacy (WEP) is kind of a security protocol for WLAN defined in the 802.11b standard. It is not that secure though as the header and the trailer are not encrypted at all. Typical security attacks against WLANs may include Eavesdropping, RF jamming, and Encryption Cracking. The list keeps growing everyday.

There are other wireless technology terms you would want to know:

Wi-Fi Protected Setup (WPS) is a standard intended for the easy and secure establishment of a wireless home network. To add a new device to the wireless network there can be four choices. They are the PIN Method, the PBC Method, the NFC Method, and the USB Method. Wireless Zero Configuration (WZC) refers to Wireless Auto Configuration (WLAN AutoConfig). It is a wireless connection management utility that comes with Windows XP and later. It works by selecting a wireless network to connect to basing on a user's preferences, even in the absence of a wireless network utility from the NIC manufacturer.

Bluejacking is all about the sending of unsolicited message over Bluetooth. Bluesnarfing describes the unauthorized access of private information from the wireless device via Bluetooth connection. Wardriving is about searching for Wi-Fi wireless networks through driving around, mostly with a portable computer or a hand held device.

A rogue access point is a Wi-Fi access point which has been installed on and running in the network without proper authorization. It needs not be of evil intent though. The bad thing about it is that it allows just about anyone equipped with an 802.11-equipped device to access mission-critical network resources. One method for detecting rogues is to use wireless sniffing tools to capture information regarding access points that are within range. A better way to detect them is to use a central console attached to the wired side of the network for monitoring. A rogue peer refers to an end-user computer that has bridging and wireless functionalities enabled.

WPA (Wi-Fi Protected Access) is an alternative WLAN security approach. It focuses on providing centralized authentication and dynamic key distribution, which is based on the IEEE 802.11 Task Group "i" end-to-end framework. WPA can provide payload integrity. WEP uses cyclic redundancy check (CRC), which is less secure with regard to payload integrity. LEAP (Lightweight Extensible Authentication Protocol) is a proprietary wireless LAN authentication method invented by Cisco. Its important features include dynamic WEP keys and mutual authentication between a wireless client and a RADIUS server.

Newer WLAN systems use a centralized controller that can configure all APs dynamically in the wireless environment. The controller can push the configuration to every single individual AP and then monitor all of them in real time. This is the preferred way of WLAN management.

One primary purpose of WIPS (wireless intrusion prevention system) is to prevent unauthorized network access to LAN by wireless devices. These systems are usually implemented as an overlay to the existing Wireless LAN infrastructure, although it could be possible to have them deployed totally standalone.

A wireless DoS attack can take place when a hacker continually bombards an AP with bogus requests. In a network injection attack, a hacker can inject bogus networking re-configuration commands into the APs for affecting other local network gears. The Caffe Latte attack aims at defeating WEP by targeting the Windows wireless stack for obtaining the WEP key from a remote client.

## WAN Networking

A WAN covers a relatively broad geographic area that often uses transmission facilities provided by common carriers. It requires quite many different devices to run, EXAMPLES: WAN switches, access servers, modems, CSU/DSUs, and ISDN terminal adapters.

A point-to-point link provides a single pre-established WAN communications path from one premise to another. You usually need to have it leased from a carrier or a service provider and thus is often called leased line.

PSTN (aka POTS plain old telephone service) provides an outdated form of point to point connection. In a PSTN the basic circuit has a 64 kilobits-p/sec channel called the DS0. Audio voice is digitized at a rate of 8 kHz via 8-bit PCM modulation. Call is switched using SS7 between telephone exchanges. Dialup services are cost-effective solutions for remote connectivity when cost is a concern and usage is not high. It is slow though (56K for dial up via the regular phone line).

Point-to-Point Protocol (PPP) is a method for connecting a computer to a remote network, over point-to-point links. It works at the data link layer, and is more stable than SLIP. Most importantly, it has error checking features included.

Many WANs deploy virtual circuits for cost sharing purpose. The two major types of virtual circuits are switched virtual circuits and permanent virtual circuits. Switched circuits allow data connections to be initiated when needed and terminated when completed. Example: ISDN. Packet switching allows users to share common carrier resources continuously without the need for connection initialization all the time. Examples include ATM, Frame Relay and X.25.

Basic Rate Interface (BRI) ISDN consists of two 64-Kbps B-channels plus one D-channel for transmitting control information. Primary Rate Interface (PRI) ISDN consists of 23 B-channels plus one D-channel in the US or 30 B-channels plus one D-channel in Europe. Cable modems are designed to operate over cable TV lines. Digital subscriber lines (DSL) are high speed last-mile technologies that use special modulation schemes to pack data onto copper wires of the traditional telephone network.

Frame Relay can support data transfer rates at 1.544 Mbps and/or 45 Mbps. It handles multiple virtual circuits using High-Level Data Link Control (HDLC) encapsulation between connected devices.

Codecs are deployed for compressing data. They are usually lossy, for achieving a relatively small file size. Lossless codecs are available, but the small increase in quality often does not worth the increase in file size. It is in fact possible to have repeated application of lossy codecs for repeated encoding and subsequent decoding, but quality will be degraded quite significantly.

## VoIP

VoIP networks rely on the H.323 standard for transmitting real-time audio communications over packet-based networks. Most VoIP implementations face problems related to latency and jitter due to the fact that UDP is deployed. A jitter buffer may be put in place to alleviate the problem. Echo can be the result of impedance mismatches in the analog circuitry, as well as acoustic coupling of signal at the receiving end.

Fixed delays are really difficult to control but a little bit of delays can be minimized through marking voice packets as delay sensitive traffic provided that you have QoS mechanism in place. On the other hand, since the primary cause of packet losses is congestion, congestion management and avoidance can be helpful.

An audio codec could be a software or a hardware or a combination of both. Do keep in mind, using digital samples to represent audio data has fundamental limitations regardless of the choice of codec. In particular, the highest possible audio frequency that may be reconstructed from digital data is at the most half the sample frequency.

## Review Questions:

1, In a VoIP implementation, echo is the result of:

2, Many WANs deploy virtual circuits for what purpose?

3, How does network injection attack work?

4, Why is WEP not too secure?

5, What is the use of a crossover cable?

6, Why is VLAN configuration highly flexible?

## Answers:

1, Most VoIP implementations face problems related to latency and jitter due to the fact that UDP is deployed. A jitter buffer may be put in place to alleviate the problem. Echo can be the result of impedance mismatches in the analog circuitry, as well as acoustic coupling of signal at the receiving end.

2, Many WANs deploy virtual circuits for cost sharing purpose. The two major types of virtual circuits are switched virtual circuits and permanent virtual circuits.

3, In a network injection attack, a hacker can inject bogus networking re-configuration commands into the APs for affecting other local network gears.

4, Wired Equivalent Privacy (WEP) is kind of a security protocol for WLAN defined in the 802.11b standard. It is not that secure though as the header and the trailer are not encrypted at all.

5, A crossover cable has the standard RJ-45 cable between source and destination cross-connected so you may connect computer to computer directly without going through a hub or a switch.

6, Since VLANs are based on logical connections, they are extremely flexible in terms of configuration and application.

# Server and network security

## Security planning

Good network security design often follows a top down approach and must reflect the goals, characteristics, and policies of the organizations in which they operate. The primary goals that drive internetworking design and implementation are application availability, cost of ownership and user satisfaction. A top down approach to network design often calls for your understanding of the constraints and objectives of network use as well as the applications and data on which the business relies upon on, before considering the viable internetworking options.

It is always recommended that you start your design effort with the business objectives because your network has the most important mission of helping users in achieving business objectives. Once these objectives are well understood, you may proceed further. You shall gain understand on the applications that will be running on the network, the systems that are attached to the network, and the data that will be flow through them.

A proper network security design and implementation plan should outline the required network design tasks on a phase by phase, step by step manner. Within each phase there should be steps that details what are to be done. The advantage of having a proper implementation plan handy is to introduce specific network benefits according to a schedule, thus allowing for proper resource allocation, planning, change control, and configuration and installation. During the design phase, a prototype may be made available for initial testing and review. Before finalizing the new design and putting it into final production use, thorough testing must be done following a well-prepared test plan.

A proper test plan should be in place to address all the key features developed in the planning phase. It should be followed to ensure compatibility with existing system performance as well as to minimize the possibility for delay-causing problems in the deployment stage.

## Equipments and devices

A packet consists of a header which marks the beginning of the packet, a payload of data, and a trailer which marks the end of the packet. The checksum if available for error checking is located at the trailer. The header has to specify the data type in transit.

A firewall prevents unauthorized access to or from a private network by examining each message and/or packet that passes through it and blocks those that do not meet the specified security criteria. A packet filter examines each packet entering or leaving the network and accepts or rejects it based on pre-defined security rules. The former uses more sophisticated mechanisms and are more dynamic in nature, but is more expensive and is more costly computing resource-wise

An application gateway applies security mechanisms to specific applications. A circuit-level gateway applies security mechanisms when a connection is established.

A proxy server intercepts all messages entering and leaving the network and make outgoing requests on behalf of users. It aims at enhancing web surfing performance.

An intrusion detection system (IDS) is a hardware and/or software which inspects all inbound and outbound network activity and identifies suspicious patterns that may indicate a network or system attack from someone attempting to break into a system. With regards to misuse detection, an IDS analyzes the information it gathers and compares it to the database of attack signatures.

A remote access server (RAS) is a special type of server that is made available specifically for handling remote users that are logging in remotely. It allows users to gain access to files and print services on your internal LAN from a remote location. Once a remote user is authenticated by the RAS server he/she may access the shared drives and printers as if he/she were physically inside the internal LAN.

A demilitarized zone (DMZ) refers to a small subnetwork that sits between your trusted internal and the public Internet. Typically, this DMZ contains network devices that are deliberately made accessible to Internet traffic, such as Web servers, FTP servers, SMTP servers ...etc.

Some firewall and proxy software can perform Network Address Translation (NAT), which allows a LAN to use one set of IP addresses for internal traffic and a second set of addresses for external traffic. This function should be located at the point where the LAN meets the WAN for effective network protection.

Keep in mind, a firewall doesn't stop viruses. Boot Sector Virus attaches itself to the boot sector of a floppy disk or an executable file and copies all or part of itself onto the boot sector of your hard drive. File-Infecting Virus attaches themselves to executable files associated with other software applications. Macro Virus affects Word and Excel templates.

## Special considerations on security and continuity

Though the benefits of modern IT systems (such as computerized membership management systems) are plentiful, the use of very advanced yet highly sophisticated technologies may present severe continuity issues. Fault-tolerant equipments do have redundant capabilities, but these capabilities won't help if the physical site is compromised (did you watch Die Hard 4.0?).

You need to consider the point(s) of failure you have. A centralized system has everything centrally managed, meaning you have a single point of failure (all risks in one place). With a distributed system you have multiple points of failure (small risks in multiple different places) that are interconnected (the connections themselves could be points of failure too). You need to achieve a proper balance between the two extremes.

Regardless of the type(s) of technology you are implementing, for the sake of security (security can affect your continuity big time) there must be a proper Information Management Policy in place. This policy should clearly define information as an asset of the business unit that needs protection, and that local business managers are the owners of information who are ultimately held responsible. In fact, to get the staff really serious about information security, it is necessary to define roles and responsibilities of those involved in the ownership and classification of information.

Identity theft occurs when someone uses another individual's personal information to take on that person's identity. This act could be much more than misuse of a name and a Social Security number as it often deals with fraudulent credit card use and mail fraud. Identity theft can become extremely easy when one's computer is being hacked into. That's why personal firewall should be used on desktop for home use.

Office personnel must be aware of the risk of Social engineering, which is a collection of techniques used to manipulate people into performing actions or divulging confidential information. While similar to a confidence trick or simple fraud, the term typically applies to trickery for information gathering or computer system access.

## Malware

Malware is software designed to infiltrate or damage a computer system without the owner's informed consent. It is a blend of the words "malicious" and "software". The expression is a general term used by computer professionals to mean a variety of forms of hostile, intrusive, or annoying software or program code. Software is considered malware based on the intent of the creator rather than any particular features. It includes computer viruses, worms, trojan horses, spyware, adware, and other unwanted software, which are quite often spread through email attachments. Some newest malware uses web site scripting languages like Javascript and Active X to carry malicious code, which could be easily downloaded through a Web browser and executed in a totally unnoticed way. Newer browsers do allow you to configure and restrict such functionalities.

## Viruses and worms

The best-known types of malware are viruses and worms, which are known for the manner in which they spread, rather than any other particular behavior. Originally, the term computer virus was used for a program which infected other executable software, while a worm transmitted itself over a network to infect computers. More recently, the words are often used interchangeably.

 NOTE: Just because you have antivirus software installed on your PC doesn't guarantee you are protected against the latest malware threats. To maintain your protection, you have to use the latest version of antivirus software available for your PC. You should also update the virus definitions daily with the LiveUpdate utility that comes with your antivirus software.

## Spyware

Spyware applications are typically bundled as a hidden component of freeware or shareware programs that can be downloaded from the Internet. Once installed, the spyware monitors user activity on the Internet and transmits that information in the background to someone else. Since spyware is using memory and system resources for its own purpose at the background, it can lead to system crashes or general system instability.

## Trojan horse

As a common type of Trojan horses, a legitimate software might have been corrupted with malicious code which runs when the program is used. The key is that the user has to invoke the program in order to trigger the malicious code. In other words, a trojan horse simply cannot operate autonomously. You would also want to know that most but not all trojan horse payloads are harmful - a few of them are harmless.

Most trojan horse programs are spread through e-mails. Some earlier trojan horse programs were bundled in "Root Kits". For example, the Linux Root Kit version 3 (lrk3) which was released in December 96 had tcp wrapper trojans included and enhanced in the kit.

## Keystroke logger

Keystroke logging (in the form of spyware) was originally a function of diagnostic tool deployed by software developers for capturing user's keystrokes. This is done for determining the sources of error or for measuring staff productivity. Imagine if someone uses it to capture user input of critical business data such as CC info ... You may want to use anti spyware applications to detect and clean them up. Web-based on-screen keyboards may be a viable option for web applications.

Keystroke Monitoring is a formal security process whereby administrators view and record the keystrokes entered by the user and the computer's immediate response. Keystroke Monitoring has to rely on keystroke logger to function though.

## Cryptography

Cryptography refers to the art and act of protecting information by transforming it into an unreadable format (the cipher text). Once encrypted, only those who possess a secret key can decipher the message back into plain text. Symmetric-key cryptography refers to an encryption system in which the sender and receiver of a message share a single, common key. Public-key cryptology, on the other hand, utilizes two keys, one refers to the public key for encrypting messages and one private key for decrypting them. Encrypted messages can sometimes be broken by cryptanalysis (codebreaking), although modern cryptography techniques are not too easy to break.

## DES

Data Encryption Standard (DES) is a popular symmetric-key encryption method standardized by ANSI. It uses a 56-bit key and the block cipher method capable of breaking text into 64-bit blocks for further encryption. 3DES is a mode of DES which encrypts data three times.

## PGP

Pretty Good Privacy (PGP) is a popular technique for encrypting email messages sent over the internet. A digital certificate is kind of an attachment to an electronic message. The primary use of it is to verify that a user sending a message is who he or she claims to be. Digital signature is data digest encrypted with the private key of the signer. It is always unique to its bearer. For digital signature to serve its purpose, both the signer and the verifier must use the same hash function to digest the data. Popular methods for producing digital signatures include RSA with SHA-1 and DSA with SHA-1.

## Disk based encryption

Whole Disk Encryption protects all data on an entire computer disk drive. The engine behinds it operates at the system level that is between the operating system and the disk drive, thus providing totally transparent sector-by-sector disk encryption in background. There are commercial software for this purpose. Windows also offer the EFS (Encryption File System) for similar use.

## EES

In the Escrowed Encryption Standard (EES), "escrow" means that something is handed over to a third person to be given to the grantee only upon the fulfillment of a condition. A key escrow system describes a system which entrusts the two components comprising a cryptographic key (i.e. the two values from which a key can be derived) to two key component holders (who are the escrow agents). The key component holders provide the components of a key to a "grantee" (such as a law enforcement official) upon fulfillment of the condition that the grantee can properly demonstrated legal authorization to conduct electronic surveillance.

The EES standard specifies the use of a symmetric-key encryption and decryption algorithm (known as SKIPJACK) and a Law Enforcement Access Field (known as LEAF) creation method for providing decryption of encrypted telecommunications during the time when interception is legally authorized. Both the SKIPJACK algorithm and the LEAF creation method are to be implemented in the electronic devices such as in the form of integration IC chips (such as the Clipper Chip). Decryption of the lawfully intercepted telecommunications can be achieved through the use of the LEAF, the decryption algorithm and the two escrowed key components.

The encryption/decryption algorithm and the LEAF creation method should only be implemented in electronic devices that are fully protected against unauthorized entry, modification, tampering and reverse engineering.

## OpenSSL

OpenSSL is a cryptography toolkit that implements the Secure Sockets Layer (SSL v2/v3) and Transport Layer Security (TLS v1) network protocols as well as other related cryptography standards that are required by them. The openssl program works in the command line envrionemnt - you may use the various cryptography functions of the crypto library from the shell. Particularly you may use it for creating RSA, DH and DSA key parameters as well as creating X.509 certificates, CSRs and CRLs; and calculating Message

Digests. You may also use it to perform encryption and decryption with Ciphers.

## P3P

The Platform for Privacy Preferences Project (P3P) is a W3C effort which enables web sites to express their privacy practices in a standard format that can be retrieved automatically and interpreted easily by the various user agent software. Agent software are supposed to be able to automate decision-making based on the P3P practices when appropriate. The goal is to make the privacy/data-gathering process more transparent.

## Access Control Models

Access control protects your systems and resources from unauthorized access. An access control model is a framework that dictates how subjects access objects. The most popular models are: mandatory access control, discretionary access control and role-based access control. Even though these models are often associated with IT technology, try to think of them as security management principles – they can be applied to disciplines other than IT.

The decision of what access control models to implement is based on organizational policy and on two generally accepted standards of practice, which are separation of duties and least privilege.

Controls may be characterized as either mandatory or discretionary. With mandatory controls, only administrators may make decisions that bear on or derive from the predefined policy. Access controls that are not based on established policy may be characterized as discretionary controls (or need-to-know controls). With the Discretionary model, the creator of a file is the 'owner' and can grant ownership to others. Access control is at the discretion of the owner. Most common implementation is through access control lists. Discretionary access control is required for the Orange Book "C" Level.

Mandatory controls are prohibitive and permissive. With the Mandatory model, control is based on security labels and categories. Access decisions are based on clearance level of the data and clearance level of the user, and, classification of the object. Rules are made by management, configured by the administrators and enforced by the operating system. Mandatory access control is required for the Orange Book "B" Level.

With the Role-Based model, access rights are assigned to roles – not directly to users. Roles are usually tighter controlled than groups - a user can only have one role. Roles can be thought of as collections of permissions to use resources appropriate to a staff's job function. This works with the assumption that all permissions needed to perform a job function can be neatly encapsulated. In fact, this is not easy. A possibly viable alternative is rule-based access control, which has access decisions made in real time by scripted policy rules. These can either be used to replace or complement the roles. You may even combine rule-based and role-based approaches in certain cases.

## ACLs VERSUS Capabilities

The two fundamental means of enforcing privilege separation and controlling access are access control lists (ACLs) and capabilities. The semantics of ACLs have been proven to be insecure in many situations. It has also been shown that ACL's promise of giving access to an object to only one person can never be guaranteed in practice. Both of these problems are resolved by capabilities. This does not mean practical flaws exist in all ACL-based systems, but only that the designers of certain utilities must take responsibility to ensure that they do not introduce flaws.

For various historical reasons, capabilities have been mostly restricted to research operating systems and commercial OSes still use ACLs. Capabilities can, however, also be implemented at the language level, leading to a style of programming that is essentially a refinement of standard object-oriented design. A reason for the lack of adoption of capabilities may be that ACLs appeared to offer a quick fix for security without pervasive redesign of the operating system and hardware.

Using Windows as an example to illustrate how ACL works:

Whenever you perform an action on an object in Windows, the action is encoded into a 32 bit integer called the ACCESS_MASK). The ACCESS_MASK is specific to the object you are trying to create. When you open the object with the requested ACCESS_MASK, Windows will get your username from your thread token and then start reading the discretionary access control list that can be obtained from the security descriptor. The DACL can be thought of as a table of user SIDs, ACCESS_MASKs, and access types. Each row in this table is called an

Access Control Entry. When an action is performed, Windows will enumerate this list to find an entry that refers to your thread token.

*Note that in Windows, a Security Identifier (SID) allows a user to be recognized by means of a hash. Discretionary Access Control List (Dacl) is where the permissions of the object are kept. On the other hand, System Access Control List (Sacl) is for specifying the type of auditing to be performed on the object.*

## Using Unix/Linux as an example to illustrate how ACL works:

On Unix and Linux, an ACL refers to the list of all the people who can read from, write to, and/or execute a particular file in your account. Every file has an ACL. To view the ACL for a particular file, you need to use the getacl command via the command known as getacl <filename>. If you wish to allow or disallow another person with an account to access the file, you use the setacl command.

## Server room configuration

Server rooms are usually soundproofed, with automatically locking doors that are never to be left propped open. For security purpose they should not have windows, viewports or false ceiling. They should have constant failsafe climate control for maintaining proper temperatures. Sprinkler systems are not installed inside as they may damage the equipments. Servers are usually mounted off the floor, and the floors are usually static-resistant and not waxed.

## Review Questions:

1, Compare packet filter with application gateway.

2, What is the benefit of using proxy service?

3, What is a DMZ?

4, What is the primary use of a digital certificate?

5, Most trojan horse programs are spread through:

6, What are the best-known types of malware?

7, How does NAT perform address translation?

## Answers:

*1, A packet filter examines each packet entering or leaving the network and accepts or rejects it based on pre-defined security rules. An application gateway applies security mechanisms to specific applications.*

*2, A proxy server intercepts all messages entering and leaving the network and make outgoing requests on behalf of users. It aims at enhancing web surfing performance.*

*3, A demilitarized zone (DMZ) refers to a small subnetwork that sits between your trusted internal and the public Internet.*

*4, A digital certificate is kind of an attachment to an electronic message. The primary use of it is to verify that a user sending a message is who he or she claims to be.*

*5, Most trojan horse programs are spread through e-mails. Some earlier trojan horse programs were bundled in "Root Kits".*

*6, The best-known types of malware are viruses and worms, which are known for the manner in which they spread, rather than any other particular behavior.*

*7, Some firewall and proxy software can perform Network Address Translation (NAT), which allows a LAN to use one set of IP addresses for internal traffic and a second set of addresses for external traffic.*

# Preparing for disasters

### Disaster Recovery Plans For Servers

Backup copies of the operating system, the application software and all the critical data must be made on a regular basis. The frequency of the backup would depend largely on the frequency of changes made as well as the criticality of the concerned data.

A backup copy of the most recent release version of the operating system and the application software should be made available during the process of rebuilding a crashed server.

Backup copies of the critical data should be made available when the current data. The data should be backed up on a frequency determined by the user. Generally, application with high transaction volume should have data backups made more frequently.

There are different backup schemes for rotating and replacing backups. A backup rotation scheme refers to a method put in place for effectively backing up data where multiple media are involved in the backup process.

- A First In, First Out FIFO backup scheme involves saving the new or modified files onto the oldest media in a set. It is very simple to use.

- A Grandfather-father-son backup method has been very popular for making tape backups. It involves defining three sets of backups, which are daily (son), weekly (father) and monthly (grand father). The son backups are rotated on a daily basis with one graduating to father status every week. The father backups are rotated on a weekly basis with one graduating to grandfather status every month.

- An incremented media method has a set of numbered media that is being used until the end of the cycle. Then the cycle is repeated using media numbered the same but incremented by one.

- The Towers of Hanoi rotation method is a recursive method which is quite complex to implement.

From a technical perspective, these backup methods are available:

- The Image/block level backup method deals with blocks of data. The backup application will open the disk as a raw disk and then perform logical block-level read and write operations. Backup and restore operations are very fast but no access is allowed during the operation.

- The Application-level backup method is usually application specific. In other words, the backup and restore operations are tightly associated with the application.

- With the Differential Backup method, a differential backup will archive all changes made since the last full backup. The backup process is fast. A full backup, in contrast, is slow to backup but convenient to restore since you only need to have one set of media available.

- File-based incremental backup is typically used when a different set of files is created or modified.

- Direct-attached backup is all about attaching storage devices to the server directly. It remains a very popular topology for backing up servers.

- Network-attached backup works in a LAN. With it, you can have a server on the LAN with a backup device that could be shared by all the servers on the LAN.

- LAN-free backup assumes that a storage area network is in place to provide a high bandwidth between any two devices and offer multiple simultaneous bandwidth capability between multiple pairs of devices.

- With server-free backup, the backup server does not need to spend much effort while the actual backup is accomplished through the data mover agent - the data is moved directly from the source to the backup media without going through the backup server.

**Change Management**

You can think of Change Management as

❖ The task of managing change

❖ An area of professional practice

❖ A body of knowledge

**You need proper change management skills to obtain buy-ins and minimize resistance. Remember, the implementation of a new security policy constitutes a change. The deployment of new security mechanisms also constitutes a change. People like to resist to changes all the time!**

One meaning of managing change refers to the making of changes in a planned and managed or systematic fashion, with the aim of more effectively implementing new methods and systems in an ongoing organization. These changes may be of the type which the organization exercises little or no control, or of the type that is well-planned.

As an "Area of Professional Practice", we see many independent consultants who acknowledge that they are change agents that manage change for their clients, that their practices are change management practices. And stemming from the view of change management as an area of professional practice, there arises the third definition of change management: the subject matter of change management as a body of knowledge.

In fact, at the heart of change management we have the change problem - some future state to be realized, some current state to be left behind, and some process for getting from the one to the other. At the conceptual level, the change problem is a matter of moving from one state to another. At the practical level, changes and the change problems they present are problems of adaptation, that they require the organization to adjust itself to an ever-changing set of circumstances.

Generally speaking, there is no single strategy in regards to change management. One may adopt a general or what is called a "grand strategy", but for any given initiative some mix of strategies is the best option.

## Change Management VS Change Control

If we play with the textual definitions, one may argue that Change Management and Change Control are two totally different disciplines. In fact, in the field of Project Management, there tend to be differing understandings of these terms or expressions. The problems are compounded where participants are unfamiliar with project work and do not recognize the implicit context.

The term Change Management is normally used to mean the achievement of change in human behavior as part of an overall business solution. The term Change Control, which is often being referred to as "Change Management", refers to the management process for requesting reviewing, approving, carrying out and controlling changes to the project's deliverables. Change Control is usually applied once the first version of a deliverable has been completed and agreed.

Sometimes people associate Change Control with Configuration Management, which is the technical and administrative control of the multiple versions or editions of a specific deliverable (particularly where the component has been changed after it was initially completed):

## Configuration Management

*"Configuration Management is the identification and maintenance of the configuration of a software product, throughout the product's life, and including both successive and parallel product versions, for the purpose of systematically controlling changes and thereby maintaining the product's integrity and traceability"*[1].

---

[1] http://www.anu.edu.au/people/Roger.Clarke/SOS/ChgeCtl90.html

In the context of IT, the term **configuration management** (configuration control) often refers to:

i, the management of security features and assurances through control of changes made to hardware, software, firmware, documentation, test, test fixtures and test documentation of an automated information system, throughout the development and operational life of a system; and

ii, the control of changes, including the recording thereof, that are made to the hardware, software, firmware, and documentation throughout the system lifecycle.

**Revision control** (also known as version control) refers to the management of multiple revisions of the same unit of information. It is most commonly used in system engineering and software development to manage ongoing development of digital documents like application source code. Changes are identified by incrementing an associated number or letter code, termed the "revision number", "revision level", or simply "revision" and associated historically with the person making the change.

**Release Management** is the discipline within software engineering of managing software releases. A release manager serves as a liaison between varying business units to guarantee smooth and timely delivery of software products or updates. He also holds the keys to production systems and takes responsibility for their quality and availability.

Best practices suggest that information security can be employed most effectively by addressing security during the design and management of applications and infrastructure. Therefore, the information security manager should ensure that the awareness of security baselines and configuration management are properly integrated early in the design and management process. He should also understand the change and configuration management activities used by the organization so that security implications can be considered and addressed.

## Preparing for emergency response

In order to enable an organization to respond to and recovery from disruptive and destructive information security events, the information security manager has to perform the following tasks:

- Develop and implement process for detecting, identifying and analyzing security-related events

- Develop response and recovery plans that include organizing, training and equipping the teams

- Ensure periodic testing of the response and recovery plans where appropriate

- Ensure the execution of response and recover plans as required

- Establish procedures for documenting an event as a basis for subsequent action including forensics when necessary

- Manage post-event reviews to identify causes and corrective actions

It is recommended that a number of different mechanisms be employed to detect security-related events such as monitoring incident reporting websites, monitoring the news organizations, monitoring user organizations and monitoring the hardware and software vendors.

Information gathered through the detection process should be assembled and organized to identify security-related events. This identification process may take place using a criteria defined by the information security manager or by following industry best practices. In any case, by categorizing and prioritizing security events, quick action can take place on the important security events without getting lost.

Common examples of security related incidents include:

- Malicious code attacks

- Unauthorized access

- Unauthorized utilization of services

- Disruption of service

- Misuse

- Espionage

- Social engineering

## Responding to incidents and managing recovery

The typical incident response goals are:

- Recovering quickly and efficiently from security incidents

- Minimizing impact of the security incident

- Responding systematically and decreasing the likelihood of reoccurrence

- Balancing operational and security

- Dealing with legal issues

Security incident types may include but are not limited to:

- Malicious code attacks

- Unauthorized access

- Disruption of services

- Misuse (intentional or unintentional)

- Espionage

- Hoaxes

- Unusual Events

- Erratic and persistent unusual system behavior

Minor incidents are those for which there are routine solutions. Medium incidents are those that do not have routine solutions but are still limited in scope and consequences. Severe incidents are those that involve significant personal data leakage, compromised institutional data, or that have the potential to impact a significant number of users, all of which can produce significant consequences.

To effectively plan for IS specific Incident Handling, follow the steps below:

1. Come up with a clear, concise statement of scope, intention and constraints.

2. Provide computing and network resource descriptions.

3. Perform an impact assessment.

4. Delegate roles and responsibilities (you can't do it all).

5. List staff and vendor contact information (in case you need outside help).

6. Be specific about your incident response actions, notifications and priorities.

7. Identify the necessary essential response resources.

8. Spell out incident investigation and documentation requirements.

9. Continually exercise, update and maintain your plan.

One critical part of handling any serious emergency situation is in the management of Disaster Recovery. Remember, the priority during recovery is ALWAYS the safety and well being of the employees and other involved persons. Other priorities include the minimization of the emergency itself, the removal or minimization of the threat of further injury or damage and the re-establishment of external services (power, telecom …etc).

Preventions against disasters may be implemented in many forms, and may make your life significantly easier during and after a disaster. Examples:

- You may have backups sent off-site weekly or even daily.

- You may use a Remote backup facility. If you have the $, you may even upgrade your network to deploy Storage Area Networks (SANs) over multiple sites so data can be made immediately available without the need to perform synchronization.

- You may use surge protectors to minimize the effect of power surges.

- You may use Uninterruptible Power Supply (UPS) to ensure continuous supply of power.

- You may set up more fire alarms and make the extinguishers more easily accessible.

- You may implement anti-virus software in your network.

- You may purchase insurance coverage on hardware or even software.

You may also specify the expected RTO. **Recovery time objective (RTO) refers to the amount of time allowed for the recovery of a business function or resource after a disaster occurs. Do note that a RTO is hardly a rigid timeline – the disaster we face could be totally different from time to time, so the same RTO may just be impossible to apply to every case.**

Recovery Time Objective (RTO) is defined as the time frame between an unplanned interruption of business operations and the resumption of business at a reduced level of service, while Recovery Point Objective (RPO) defines how much work in progress can be lost.

Generally speaking, the goals of RTO and RPO are not tightly coupled, nor are they completely decoupled. They should be determined independently, although it may be determined at some later point that they are interrelated due to infrastructure or technology issues.

## Risk Management

Risk Profile describes the broad parameters one should consider in executing its business strategy. Risk Appetite refers to the level of uncertainty one is willing to assume given the corresponding reward. Risk Tolerance is different - it entails a stated max amount of risk one is willing to keep in executing its business strategy.

Risk analysis refers to the process of analyzing a target environment and the relationships of its risk-related attributes, with the goal of identifying threat vulnerabilities and associating these vulnerabilities with affected assets. Additionally, the potential for and nature of any undesirable result as well as different risk-reducing countermeasures are fully evaluated.

Risk assessment, on the other hand, represents the assignment of value to assets, threat frequency on annualized basis, consequence and exposure factors, and other elements of chance. Risk assessment techniques may be qualitative or quantitative. They may also be described in terms of the degree to which factors such as asset value, exposure factor, and threat frequency are assigned quantitative values.

Consequence assessment estimates the degree of harm or loss that could occur. Threat Identification identifies threat, which is an entity or event with the potential to harm. Vulnerability Analysis deals with vulnerability, which is a condition or weakness in security procedures that could be exploited by a threat.

Likelihood Assessment estimates the frequency or chance of a threat happening. It considers the presence, tenacity, and strengths of threats as well as the effectiveness of safeguards or presence of vulnerabilities. Risk mitigation involves the selection and implementation of controls to reduce risk to a level acceptable to management.

Certain risk analysis tools are of a quantitative nature, which helps the analytical process to a certain extent. For example, with a Risk Metrics, there are six primitive elements that should be treated quantitatively:

- Asset Value – the financial value of your critical tangible/intangible assets

- Threat Frequency – how frequent could this happen?

- Threat Exposure Factor – what is the magnitude of loss?

- Safeguard Effectiveness – are the safeguards really useful?

- Safeguard Cost – how much would these safeguards cost?

- Uncertainty – are you sure of your estimates? Would there be surprises of any sort?

Strategic risk assessment plays a significant role in the risk mitigation process by helping to avoid uninformed risk acceptance and having, later, to retrofit necessary risk mitigating measures. Sadly, management often is ignorant of the risk assessment process, the real nature of the risks, and the benefits of risk assessment. With properly implemented risk assessment plans and measures, you may promote a strategic approach to risk management by helping management to understand:

1. What is at risk?

2. The value at risk

3. The kinds of threats that could occur and their consequences annualized and expressed in $.

4. What can be done to reduce risk? And what is the cost?

## Loss Calculations

The 3 major loss calculation models are:

- Single Loss Expectancy (SLE)

- Annualized Loss Expectancy (ALE)

- Cumulative Loss Expectancy (CLE)

NOTE: Loss reduction aims at lessening the exposure to a particular risk. It involves planning for, and reacting to, a damaging event so to limit the impact. Insurance policies and evacuation procedures are typical examples of loss reduction mechanisms.

The Single Loss Expectancy model is the model upon which the Annualized Loss Expectancy and Cumulative Loss Expectancy models are based. This simple (and less accurate) model has its roots in accounting, with the purpose of determining how much value in terms of dollars will be lost, and is often used to express the results in a financial impact analysis.

The Annualized Loss Expectancy Model of risk comes closer (relatively) to painting an accurate picture of risk by adding the probability of an event happening over a single year's time. To reach an answer, you need to first calculate the Single Loss Expectancy to determine this value. Then you obtain the product of the Single Loss Expectancy and the value of the asset to produce the Annualized Loss Expectancy. The formula looks like this:

| Single Loss Loss | | Annualized Rate | | Annualized |
|---|---|---|---|---|
| Expectancy | x | of Occurrence | = | Expectancy |

The Cumulative Loss Model approaches risks by taking into account all of the bad things that are likely to happen to your business over the next year. You will need to look at each threat, the probability of each threat against your business, and then derive an expected loss. You can take all of the threats, and compute the annual rate of each threat occurring.

Other terms you may want to know:

- The **Annualized rate of occurrence (ARO)** characterizes the frequency with which a threat is expected to occur on an annualized basis.

- The **Exposure factor (EF)** represents a measure of the magnitude of loss or impact on the value of an asset. It is expressed as a percent of asset value loss arising from a threat event.

# Contingency and continuity

Contingency planning is the management process for ensuring that adequate arrangements are made in anticipation of a crisis, that adequate follow-up actions are undertaken and that subsequent revisions of plans are made. It involves analyzing potential emergencies and their impact on human and ecosystems; prioritizing potential areas of intervention; developing appropriate plans and procedures to deal with prioritized emergencies; ensuring that necessary measures and follow-up actions are taken; and ensuring the availability of adequate human and financial resources. Generally speaking, contingency planning focuses more on sudden emergency scenarios that might get people caught in surprises.

Business Continuity comprises all additional plans and procedures to ensure the continuity of business operations at the company's site and its satellite locations in the event of an incident leading to the partial or complete closure of these facilities.

In short, a business continuity plan is required to permit an organization to resume operations as quickly as possible given the scope and severity of the significant disruption. As an example, the business continuity plan of a major assets management firm seeks to address the following: data back up and recovery; all mission critical systems; financial and operational assessments; alternative communications with customers, employees, and regulators; alternate physical location of employees; critical suppliers, contractor, bank impact; regulatory reporting; and assuring our customers prompt access to their funds and securities if we are unable to continue our business.

## BCP, DRP and COOP

Business continuity is a term that describes the processes and procedures an organization puts in place to ensure that essential functions can continue during and after a disaster. Business continuity planning seeks to prevent interruption of mission-critical services, and to reestablish full functioning as swiftly and smoothly as possible.

From a practical standpoint, you must understand that it may not be practical for any but the largest business functions to maintain full functioning throughout a disaster crisis. You cannot afford to keep everything running non-stop due to the high cost involved. In fact, the very first step in business continuity planning is deciding which of the organization's functions are essential, and apportioning the available budget accordingly.

Disaster Recovery Plan DRP is an approved written plan that is used to develop processes and prepare the resources, actions, tasks, and data required to facilitate recovery from any disaster or emergency. You usually have a Disaster Recovery Planning Manager assigned to oversee the creation, implementation, testing, periodic review and distribution of the DRP.

BCP is of broader scope. It deals not only with recovery but also focuses on a longer term and a broader basis of running the organization. In any case, both the BCP and the DRP contains proprietary company information and is therefore not for general distribution. Each individual possessing a copy should be responsible for maintaining it in a secure location, and in accordance with company policies for the protection of proprietary information.

Through a Continuity of Operations Plan (COOP) you ensure that your organization can continue to perform its duties and responsibilities towards its mission, even in the event of any disruption in normal working conditions.

A COOP is designed to help maintain the continuity of essential operations/functions during various potential scenarios or events, including emergencies such as fire, storm, and natural disasters, terrorist activities, power outages, or other short or long-term disruptions in the physical environment in which employees operate.

A COOP is also intended to provide a framework for staff to cover any disruption in the work production of any individual employee for any reason. Just like a BCP, a COOP is a living document that must be updated, reviewed and  practiced to remain an effective plan. All staff should be familiar with its contents, and that copies of the document should be made available at the homes and offices of all employees.

## Service Level Agreement, Disclaimer and the Warranty/Liability terms

A service-level agreement SLA is a contract element. With it, the level of service is formally defined. A customer-based SLA is an agreement with an individual customer group which covers all the services consumed. A service-based SLA covers those services being delivered by the service provider only. A multilevel SLA has the SLA split into different levels.

Below shows the major section of a real world SLA (use this as an example for learning only!):

## EXAMPLE General Term of the Service Level Agreement

This Service Level Agreement (SLA) documents the agreement between the client and XXX PROVIDER for delivery of services including services delivered, levels of service, communications, and pricing. All terms are in effect until modified by an amendment. Either party can terminate this agreement in whole or in part with 30 days notice. Billing rates may be adjusted based on service level changes. The SLA is reviewed on its anniversary.

## EXAMPLE Warranty and Liability Terms

We commit to protecting the equipment and data supported under this SLA from deliberate damage from XXX PROVIDER or other persons provided access to the equipment by XXX PROVIDER. However, we will not be held liable for and damage to equipment owned by the Department or data loss that occurs due to accidental actions by XXX PROVIDER staff or other persons.

## EXAMPLE System Availability Definitions

Systems will be available 7X24 except for regularly scheduled maintenance downtime. The standard downtime maintenance schedule is 4am to 7am on Wednesdays, other windows will be negotiated with each client and will occur between 7am and 7pm. Clients will be given at least three (3) business days notice of any scheduled downtime. There maintenance windows scheduled by the University for network and firewall changes (i.e. Thursday 4am to 7am).

XXX PROVIDER staff services will be available during normal business hours, Monday through Friday, 8am to 5pm unless otherwise specified. Severity Level 1 outages will be responded to 7X24 for critical business systems.

## EXAMPLE System Monitoring Terms

Basic operational monitoring, periodic testing of systems for proper functioning, is provided for all managed systems housed in the Data Center. The monitoring system pages the on-call systems administrator when error conditions are detected.

External operating monitoring can be arranged with the client paying the fees (approximately $22/month/url) for this service.

## EXAMPLE Problem Severity and Response Time

XXX PROVIDER Data Center will respond to problems according to the following severity levels:

| Problem Severity | Initial Response Time | Follow-up w/Client |
|---|---|---|
| Level 0 – normal business hours | Respond to client within 40 minutes of notification 100% of the time. | Hourly |
| Level 1 - off hours | Respond to client within 1.5 hour of notification 95% of the time | Hourly |

| Level 2 - normal business hours | Respond to client within 3 hours of notification 100 % of the time | Daily |
|---|---|---|
| Level 3 – normal business hours | Respond to client within 2 working days of notification 100% of the time | Weekly |

## EXAMPLE Disclaimer

A liability of the provider for noncompliance with the service level is only given if XXX Provider is solely responsible for the noncompliance. The liability applies especially not to:

- Deficiencies, for which XXX Provider is not directly accountable...
- Deficiencies caused by customers...
- Deficiencies resulting from incorrect usage of customer-owned software...
- Deficiencies that have been misleadingly reported to the customer by internal or external monitoring services...
- Deficiencies that have been caused by maintenance hours and scheduled or unscheduled maintenance work by XXX Provider or its suppliers...

If XXX Provider can prove for any asserted claim by a customer that it is no valid warranty claim, the error diagnostics and trouble shooting will be at the expense of the customer.

## EXAMPLE Severability Clause

Should any individual provisions of this Service Level Agreement be or become invalid, either in part or in full, or impracticable, this will not affect the validity of the individual contracts' other provisions. The same will also apply in the event of any unintended omissions. The invalid or impracticable provision or the omission will be replaced by a ruling that is as close as possible in economic purpose to the invalid or impracticable provision, which would have been agreed upon by both parties.

## Review Questions:

1, Describe Business continuity.

2, Describe Contingency planning.

3, Compare consequence assessment with likelihood assessment.

4, What is the difference between Risk Profile and Risk Appetite?

5, What is Change Control?

6, Compare RTO with RPO.

## Answers:

*1, Business continuity is a term that describes the processes and procedures an organization puts in place to ensure that essential functions can continue during and after a disaster.*

*2, Contingency planning is the management process for ensuring that adequate arrangements are made in anticipation of a crisis, that adequate follow-up actions are undertaken and that subsequent revisions of plans are made.*

*3, Consequence assessment estimates the degree of harm or loss that could occur. Likelihood Assessment estimates the frequency or chance of a threat happening.*

*4, Risk Profile describes the broad parameters one should consider in executing its business strategy. Risk Appetite refers to the level of uncertainty one is willing to assume given the corresponding reward.*

*5, The term Change Control, which is often being referred to as "Change Management", refers to the management process for requesting reviewing, approving, carrying out and controlling changes to the project's deliverables.*

*6, Recovery Time Objective (RTO) is defined as the time frame between an unplanned interruption of business operations and the resumption of business at a reduced level of service, while Recovery Point Objective (RPO) defines how much work in progress can be lost.*

# Physical security for computer equipments

## General guidelines

Effective physical security measures aim at protecting against unauthorized access, damage, or interference in areas where critical or sensitive information is processed, or where information processing services supporting key business functions are run.

Generally speaking, the following guidelines should always be adhered to:

- The requirements and placement of each physical security barrier should be determined basing on the value of the information or service being protected. They do have to be located away from hazardous processes and/or materials.
- Physical information processing resources must be housed in a secure area capable of protecting the resources from unauthorized physical access, fire, flooding, explosions, and other kinds of disaster.
- Only authorized personnel should be allowed entry into areas that house critical or sensitive information or information processing resources. Facilities where access by unauthorized personnel is to be prevented should require that ID badges be made visible at all times. Personnel should challenge strangers and report their presence to security. Visitors should be escorted only by authorized personnel.
- The award and distribution of passes must be strictly controlled and subject to frequent review. Quarterly reviews have to be performed to ensure that only those individuals with a job related need have access to the computing facilities. Whenever individuals change jobs, their access must be immediately barred.
- Clear Desk Policy should be promoted. Papers and discs should be stored in cabinets when not in use. Sensitive business information

should be locked away. Devices for network access should be protected by key locks, passwords and the like (best to have various methods combined). Information processing equipment and media containing highly restricted and confidential data must never be left unattended in public places.

- Off premise devices with classified information must be protected with the proper form of access protection such as passwords, smart cards, and encryption ...etc. Damaged storage devices should either be repaired or thoroughly destroyed.

- Adequate power supplies and auxiliary power supplies must be made ready. Uninterruptible Power Source (UPS) should be used to support critical information processing equipments. Power and communications lines should be subject to adequate protection. Cables and cords must be protected from unauthorized interception or damage.

- Air-conditioning units must be sufficient to support the equipments as heat is a huge concern.

- The minimum-security protection activities recommended by the vendor/manufacturer must be implemented.

- Physical emergency procedures must be clearly documented and must be regularly practiced.

- Both manually activated and automatically activated fire suppression equipment must be made ready. If automatic fire suppression system employs water, careful tuning must be performed to avoid damage to critical computer equipments.

- Fire extinguishers should be conveniently placed and well marked. Check them on a periodic basis as they all have expiration dates.


**Physical site preparation and management**

As most of the critical IT equipments are normally housed in a data centre or computer room, careful site preparation of the data centre or computer room is highly important. Site preparation should at the least cover the following aspects:

• Site selection
• Power supply
• Air conditioning and ventilation
• Fire protection and detection
• Water damage and flood control
• Physical entry control

IT operations centers should be equipped with an alternative power source which is independent of the local power grids. This may be provided through a combination of a battery-based uninterruptible power supply and a generator powered by gasoline or fuel. IT operations centers should also be equipped with independent telecommunication feeds from different vendors. Wiring configurations must be able to support rapid switching from one provider to another. In fact management is recommended to document wiring strategies and organize cables with labels or color-codes to facilitate easy troubleshooting, repair, and upgrade.

Every operations center should have adequate heating, ventilation, and air conditioning (HVAC) systems. HOWEVER, personnel should also be able to function in the event utility service is interrupted. All IT operations centers should be equipped with heat and smoke detectors installed in the ceiling, in exhaust ducts, and under raised flooring. Detectors, however, should not be situated near air conditioning vents or intake ducts.

At least one telephone line (those that would function if when power is off) must be installed in each of the console area and help desk area inside the computer room, production control office and operation management/support office.

## Fire protection

A fire fighting party should be organized in each operating shift with well-defined responsibility assigned. Regular fire drills must be carried out to allow the officers to practice the routines to be followed when fire breaks out.

Hand-held fire extinguishers should be in strategic locations in the computer area. They should be tagged for inspection and inspected at least annually. Smoke detectors could be installed to supplement the fire suppression systems. You want them to be located above and below the ceiling tiles throughout the computer area and below the raised computer room floor. Additionally, heat detectors if available should be located below the ceiling tiles in the computer area. These detectors should produce audible alarms when triggered.

Gas-based fire suppression systems are always preferred. However, if water-based systems are to be used, dry-pipe sprinkling systems would be preferred over ordinary water sprinkler systems.

*Several strategies are available for fire suppression. One of the more widely used systems in the past was a halon gas system that deprived a fire of oxygen. Newer systems rely on the same theory, but use inert agents such as Inergen, FM-200, FE-13, and carbon dioxide. Quite many facilities continue to rely on water as a fire suppressant (either a wet-pipe or a dry-pipe configuration). Problem with wet-pipe is that the pipes are filled with water and may be subject to leakage. Ideally the fire suppression system should allow operators time to shut down computer equipment and cover it with waterproof covers prior to releasing the suppressant.*

## Maintenance and testing

Preventive maintenance on equipment will for sure minimize equipment failure and can lead to early detection of potential problems. This includes minor maintenance such as cleaning peripheral equipment as well as more extensive maintenance provided by the manufacturer, vendor, or maintenance contractor. Do note that computer operators should not repair equipment or perform other than the most routine maintenance. This is due to the fact that many hardware and software warranties disclaim liability for unauthorized maintenance or alteration.

Proper cleaning procedures for the computer room must also be established. Such procedures must include at least the following:

• Regular cleaning of the external surfaces of the peripherals by operators;
• Daily emptying of the waste paper bin;
• Daily vacuum cleaning of the computer room floor;
• Daily mopping of the computer room raised floor (if any);
• Periodic cleaning of the water pipes (if any);
• Periodic cleaning of the in-house partitions, doors, lighting fixture and furniture;
• Periodic inspection and cleaning of the floor void.

You must regularly inspect the computer room to ensure the cleaning procedures are followed. Unused peripherals or equipment should be disposed of or written offs. Hardware or workstation should be well covered when there is any cleaning or maintenance work that causes a lot of dust arouse. Eating and drinking in the computer room should be avoided. Smoking in the computer room must be strictly prohibited.

Regular maintenance and testing should be arranged for all service utilities including air conditioning equipment, fire detection and prevention system, standby power supply system, power conditioning system, water sensing system and temperature sensing system. All maintenance work carried out must be recorded. AND, apart from the service utilities, emergency exits, locks and alarms must also be regularly checked.

## Equipment and Media Management

Proper controls must be implemented when taking IT equipment away from sites. For hand carry type of IT equipment such as laptop computers and mobile devices, you should consider keeping an authorized equipment list and periodically perform inventory check to check the status of such IT equipment. For fixture type of IT equipment, you may want to adopt a check-in check-out process or inventory documentation measures to identify which IT equipment has been taken away.

Proper procedures must be established for the storing and handling of backup media. Backup media containing business essential and/or mission critical information should be stored at a secure and safe location remote from the site of the equipment. Access to the backup media should only be done via a designated staff as far as possible. Movement of media IN/OUT of a library or off-site storage should be properly logged. Unless permission is granted, any staff should not be allowed to leave the computer room with any media. To facilitate the detection of loss of media, the storage rack can indicate some sort of markings/labels at the vacant slot positions. Periodic inventory check would be necessary to detect any loss or destruction.

Transportation of backup media/manuals to and from off-site must be properly handled. The cases used for carrying the media should be shockproof, heatproof, water-resistant and should be able to withstand magnetic interference. In addition, there must be consideration on protecting the media from theft, such as through encrypting the data in the storage media splitting the media into multiple parts and transported by different people.

All media containing classified information must be handled strictly in accordance with the established procedures. The construction of external media library must have the same fireproof rating as the computer room. In fact, the rating for fireproof safe for keeping vital media must reach the standard for keeping magnetic media.

To safeguard tape contents from being erased when a tape is accidentally mounted for use, all write-permit rings should be removed from the tapes on the tape racks. Physical disposal of computer equipment containing non-volatile data storage capabilities must be checked and examined to ensure all information has been removed. Destruction, overwriting or reformatting of media must be approved and performed with appropriate facilities or techniques.

## Review Questions:

1, Site preparation would cover:

2, What are the aims of physical security measures?

3, Why would you want to carry out regular fire drills?

## Answers:

*1, Site preparation should at the least cover the following aspects:*

- *Site selection*
- *Power supply*
- *Air conditioning and ventilation*
- *Fire protection and detection*
- *Water damage and flood control*
- *Physical entry control*

*2, Effective physical security measures aim at protecting against unauthorized access, damage, or interference in areas where critical or sensitive information is processed, or where information processing services supporting key business functions are run.*

*3, Regular fire drills must be carried out to allow the officers to practice the routines to be followed when fire breaks out.*

# System Implementation & Maintenance

## Special considerations

Generally speaking, when implementing servers you want to anticipate the factors of performance, cost, reliability as well as ownership and responsibility. Performance may best be characterized by response time. Cost wise you want to minimize the number of servers. You do want your servers to be reliable. If possible they should be placed near the local support resources. Note that IT organizations usually place the backbone servers in data centers with proper environmental controls, uninterrupted power supplies, and a 24-hour support team. Locating critical server resources in a controlled environment can isolate the servers from external threats and can shorten the time necessary to recover from sudden failure.

## Service packs and patches

Your OS and/or your firewall may require patching in order to stay secured. For example, Microsoft release patches to fix vulnerabilities or add security features. Patches should be applied in a consistent and repeatable manner, because failing to patch even a few computers means that the overall network is still vulnerable.

Service packs typically include all the essential patching components bundled together for easy downloading. Typically, each new service pack contains all the fixes that are included in previous service packs plus any new fixes, so most of the time you would not need to install a previous service pack before you install the latest one. Do keep in mind, patches may not work perfectly in every environment. Therefore, you should thoroughly test any patches before installing in your environment. To be secure and safe, you might want to have a plan of action to restore the system to its original state if something goes wrong. Backup should be made almost mandatory in such a plan.

## Cleaning

Dust and lint will clog the cooling vents of the computer system. This can be deadly as heat is often the biggest cause of component failure. Regular cleaning can and will for sure save you costly maintenance fees in the long run.

One suggested way to clean is to use compressed air. You may blow compressed air around the components while keeping the nozzle at least four inches away. You may particularly blow air into the power supply and into the cooling fan.

Beware of ESD when opening up the computer. ESD (Electrostatic Discharge) refers to the rapid transfer of electrostatic charge between two objects. It is the main cause of device failure.

## Windows networking

Server Message Block (SMB) is the protocol deployed by Windows for file sharing and other communications. It serves as the basis for NetBIOS communications and resources sharing over the network. SMB traffic stays in LAN only.

Share permissions apply only when a user is accessing a file or folder non-locally. They can be applied on a user or on a group level, although assigning permissions on a group basis is always recommended. Individual permissions and group permissions can be combined to form the user's effective permissions. NTFS permissions allow you to assign permissions more granularly at the folder and file level while Share permissions are limited to the folder level only. Keep in mind, file permissions always take precedence over folder permissions.

Event Viewer is the interface for managing event logging in Windows. The primary types of log are System logs, Application logs and Security logs. It is always advised that you focus on monitoring failed login/access attempts.

Single sign-on (SSO) refers to the kind of access control method which enables a user to authenticate once and gain access to network resources of other software systems. Kerberos is an authentication protocol in use by the newer Windows Servers (since Windows 2000) for facilitating the implementation of SSO.

SNMP is deployed by many network management systems for monitoring network-attached devices for conditions that warrant administrative attention. The SNMP protocol itself does not define which information a managed system should offer. Instead, it relies on the various management information bases (MIBs) to do the job. The Microsoft SMS (System Management Server) makes extensive use of SNMP. The community string serves as kind of a "password" for SNMP communication. Do note that the use of SNMP will increase network load quite a bit.

On a Windows network with Active Directory enabled, information necessary for authentication is stored in the directory – that is, each Domain Controller holds a copy – information is replicated across the entire network domain. If you have multiple domain controllers up and running, server failure would not disrupt authentication unless all domain controllers within a domain fail altogether.

## Linux networking

Linux files are setup with three types of access, which are read, write and execute. Each file belongs to a specific user and group. The term "other" generally refers to someone who is not the user (owner) of the file.

File names are made up of up to 256 characters (including "-", "_", and "."). With a long file listing you may see 10 characters that are on the left that indicate type and permissions of the file: example drwerwerwe. Character 1 is the type of file, which - is ordinary, d is directory, and l is link. Characters 2-4 show owner permissions, with character 2 indicating read permission, character 3 indicating write permission, and character 4 indicating execute permission. Characters 5-7 show group permissions (5=read, 6=write, 7=execute). Characters 8-10 show permissions for all other users (8=read, 9=write, 10=execute). There are 5 possible characters in the permission fields, which are:

r = read
w = write

x = execute
s = setuid

syslog refers to the standard for forwarding log messages. This works primarily in an IP network. The syslog protocol is a client server protocol. RMON (Remote Network MONitoring) supports monitoring and protocol analysis of LANs.

## Review Questions:

1, Some say that service packs are always cumulative. Why?

2, Which protocol is deployed by network management systems for monitoring network-attached devices?

3, On a Windows PC, what are the primary types of log? What utility can you use to view them?

## Answers:

*1, Typically, each new service pack contains all the fixes that are included in previous service packs plus any new fixes, so most of the time you would not need to install a previous service pack before you install the latest one.*
*2, SNMP is deployed by many network management systems for monitoring network-attached devices for conditions that warrant administrative attention.*
*3, Event Viewer is the interface for managing event logging in Windows. The primary types of logs are System logs, Application logs and Security logs.*

# End of book

Made in the USA
Lexington, KY
30 January 2012